MY LAST DRINK
32 stories of recovering alcoholics

Edited by

ROSS FITZGERALD and NEAL PRICE

Connor Court Publishing

Published in 2022 by Connor Court Publishing Pty Ltd

Copyright © Ross Fitzgerald and Neal Price (as a collection)

All rights reserved. No part of this book may be reproduced or transmitted in any form or by any means, electronic or mechanical, including photocopying, recording or by any information storage and retrieval system, without prior permission in writing from the publisher.

Connor Court Publishing Pty Ltd
PO Box 7257
Redland Bay QLD 4165
sales@connorcourt.com
www.connorcourtpublishing.com.au
Phone 0497-900-685

Printed in Australia

ISBN: 9781922815224

Front cover by Paige Hally

Printed in Australia

The editors would like to thank the contributors to this book for their generous and spirited story telling. Thank you also to Gerard Henderson for advice; Paige Hally for cover design; and Kaz Knights for editing assistance.

This book is dedicated to Emerald, Ava, and Kaz

In the spirit of reconciliation the editors acknowledge the Traditional Custodians of Country throughout Australia and their connections to land, sea and community. We pay our respect to their Elders past and present and extend that respect to all Aboriginal and Torres Strait Islander peoples.

Introduction

Ross Fitzgerald and Neal Price

When, decades ago, Australian hotels closed at 6:00 pm, and the public bar was only open to men, creating the notorious six o'clock swill, the pub manager or owner would always call; "Time Gentlemen please. Last Drinks. Hurry along now."

The notion of Last Drinks has entered deeply into the Australian lexicon, but there is another kind of Last Drink, the last one that an alcoholic takes before she or he gets sober. *My Last Drink* is a collection of inspiring and hitherto unpublished stories, original for this book, that canvass and explain how thirty-two recovering alcoholics managed to stop drinking and to stay stopped.

Alcoholism affects people from all walks of life irrespective of age, social standing, race, gender, sexuality, disability, or religion. This anthology includes builders, novelists, journalists, artists, lawyers, musicians, folk singers, therapists, nurses, bus drivers, accountants, police officers, web designers, and army personnel from across Australia. Eighteen men and fourteen women tell their personal stories of the last 24 hours of their alcoholic drinking.

In this book, the word 'sober' means free of alcohol and other drugs. As Ross Fitzgerald puts it, "These days, as a long-time member of Alcoholics Anonymous, I have nothing in my blood but blood."

Since its inception in America in 1935 (the first AA meetings occurred in Australia in 1945), members used only first names to identify themselves. This was a protective strategy. Given the social stigma of being an alcoholic or addict at the time, anonymity was seen as a necessary way to protect a person's privacy.

The use of nicknames developed to identify long-term members based on their character traits, has helped to form a unique fellowship. In Australia, the names Antique Harry, Circus Lil, Eight O'Clock Ross, Adequate from Arncliffe, Bow-tie Frank, Breathless Beryl, Broken Hill Jack and his brother Raucous Dick (who had no sense of volume), were and are well-known members of the AA fellowship.

In *My Last Drink* some contributors are identified by their full names e.g. Tim Olsen, Di Young, and Richard Whittaker, while other contributors have chosen to be identified by their first name, plus the first initial of their surname e.g. Fred T, Kaz K, David B. This is a personal choice enabling contributors to have control over their own story and how it is presented.

It is important to understand that there are no rules in Alcoholics Anonymous. Indeed, the only requirement for membership is, "A desire to stop drinking," no matter how slim that desire is. The Twelve Steps and Twelve Traditions of AA are in no way mandatory; they are only suggested. This includes the tradition of anonymity.

In AA, alcoholism is treated as a health problem, not a moral problem. Hence, alcoholics are not regarded as bad people who need to get good, but sick people who can recover, if we don't pick up that first drink of alcohol, one day at a time.

Alcoholism is a disease of denial and resistance. A psychiatrist once asked Ross to visit an alcoholic patient at the Wesley Hospital in Brisbane. When drunk, he tried to kill himself with a shotgun. He had blown one arm off and part of his abdomen. In the hope that he might identify, Ross told part of his drinking story. Within minutes the patient put up his remaining hand and said "If I ever get as bad as you Ross, I'll give it up." On a documentary filming trip in far north Queensland, the film crew arrived at a local pub in a small country town. The licensee's wife nervously admitted to having locked the publican in the toilet to prevent him from drinking. In his delirium he had attempted to eat the astro-turf in the toilet. When Ross suggested he go to an AA meeting, his wife said "Oh, he's not that bad."

In Alcoholics Anonymous there is room for everyone, no matter how far down the scale of life they have gone. Members include firm and tepid believers in a higher power, as well as agnostics and atheists, of whom in the fellowship there are many, including both contributing editors to this book.

The AA program is in the broadest sense a spiritual program, but not a religious one. In our experience, over the long-term most alcoholics cannot stop drinking and stay stopped through an exercise of the will. That is why a number of sober alcoholics regard the meetings of Alcoholics Anonymous which they attend as being something greater than their isolated self.

As the Swiss psychoanalyst, Carl Jung wrote to the co-founder of Alcoholics Anonymous, Bill Wilson, on January 30, 1961, the most helpful motto for an alcoholic is *"Spiritus contra spiritum"* i.e. spirit against spirit, power against power. Jung thought that to get and stay sober, alcoholics need to find something more powerful than alcohol. For many of us, that power is to be found in AA itself.

There are no dues or fees for AA membership. Moreover, no-one can be expelled from AA, which has no bosses. Indeed, in our opinion, Alcoholics Anonymous is a prime example of (peaceful) anarchism in action.

The contributing editors of *My Last Drink* are both sober alcoholics. Ross Fitzgerald has been sober for 52 years, Neal Price for 39 years. They both still regularly attend meetings of Alcoholics Anonymous.

The truth is that AA helps tens of thousands of alcoholics recover from a seemingly hopeless condition. This is demonstrated by Professor George Vaillant's path-breaking book, *The Natural History of Alcoholism Revisited*, published by Harvard University Press.

A leading American psychiatrist, Professor Vaillant's longitudinal study demonstrates that, even though it is difficult for alcoholics to stop drinking and stay stopped, AA is by far the most effective agency in helping alcoholics to recover. So as Ross and Neal often say to newcomers, and to their families, "Why not avail yourself of the best?"

Three of Ross's 43 books are about alcoholism and AA. These are his two memoirs, *Fifty Years Sober: An Alcoholic's Journey* and *My Name is Ross*, plus *Under the Influence: A History of Alcohol in Australia*, co-authored with Brisbane-based Dr Trevor Jordan.

As thousands of Australians are either sober alcoholics themselves or relatives and friends of alcoholics who are sober or trying to get sober, we are hoping that avid readers, and especially those interested in alcoholism and addiction, will find *My Last Drink* to be intellectually helpful and practically useful.

At the very least, we hope that this illuminating anthology might encourage people, whose drinking is getting out of control, to attend some meetings of AA, most of which are open to everyone, and available throughout Australia.

Our advice to a prospective newcomer is two-fold. Ask yourself a simple question: "Is alcohol costing you more than money?" and if the answer is yes, go to one or two AA meetings and try to listen for the similarities, not the differences. There is unambiguous proof that AA works. For anyone with a problem with the booze, joining this remarkable fellowship could be a life-changing decision.

As Ross and Neal have been sober buddies for almost 40 years, it has been an enjoyable and exhilarating experience working together on this fascinating project.

Ross Fitzgerald AM is Emeritus Professor of History & Politics at Griffith University and the author or co-author of 43 books. His most recent books are a memoir *Fifty Years Sober: An Alcoholic's Journey* and the co-authored political satires, *The Dizzying Heights and The Lowest Depths*, published by Hybrid in Melbourne. Professor Fitzgerald now lives in Redfern, Sydney.

Neal Price is an artist and writer who now lives in Hobart, Tasmania. He has long been engaged in the Community Cultural Development sector, with a focus on disability, mental health, ageing and oral histories.

1

Ross Fitzgerald

My last drink of alcohol was at the same place as where, when I was barely fourteen, I had my first one. This was at Her Majesty's Hotel in South Yarra. Commonly called Maisies, it was very close to Melbourne Boys High School at which, in 1958, I'd just begun Third Form.

My first alcoholic drink was about eleven in the morning, after I'd had a medical appointment (in those days I went to the doctors a lot). Because it seemed romantic and exotic, I asked for a Brandy, Lime, and Soda. In response, the bar person, who was a drag queen, said, "Yes my dear. But could you take your school cap off first?"

I first came across Alcoholics Anonymous in 1969 when I was in Cleveland, Ohio. This was after I had been hospitalised six times there, in the one mental institution – always for alcoholism and drug addiction. In my case, because I was and am needle-phobic, I never shot up. Unlike most of my friends who died of HIV and various forms of hepatitis, this almost certainly saved my life. But as well as drinking huge quantities of alcohol at any time of the day and night, I was then also consuming up to twenty barbiturates a day. Mixing so many tablets with so much alcohol resulted in speeding me up, not calming me down. Each time I was admitted to the mental hospital, I was administered a lot of Electroconvulsive Therapy (ECT), which I note is making a comeback.

Yet, despite getting myself and those close to me into terrible trouble, it had never occurred to me, until the very day that I was introduced to AA, to do anything about my drinking. This was until, after all the women in my life had given up on me, I finished up living in 'Little Italy' in Cleveland with an old railway worker named Bill, who was a bender drinker. What little food we ate, he cooked. One day after we'd cleaned our teeth, and vomited simultaneously, I said without a touch of irony: "We've got to stop cleaning our teeth mate, because every time we do, we get crook."

I'd had auditory hallucinations and heard voices since I was sixteen or seventeen, but this was the first time that I saw the animals. Bill was away on a drinking jag and, that night, the ceiling of my room came down, the walls moved in on me, and a pack of salivating Alsatian dogs were trying to devour me.

I'm a living example that you can be drunk and terrified.

And for the first time in my young life, I was still only twenty-four, a thought entered my brain; "Roscoe, it mightn't be a bad idea to do something about your drinking, for a while." So instead of hitting myself with some rotgut wine and a handful of pills, I swallowed some barbiturates and stumbled down to the bar that I was allowed to drink in each morning before it officially opened. Feeling very sorry for myself, I used to sit on my own and weep drunkenly, while on the jukebox I'd listen to songs like 'Desolation Row' and 'I'm a Nowhere Man.' It was a noon to midnight bar, located in the main road, Euclid Avenue, where the famous football team, the Cleveland Browns drank. The barman, Jimmy Jukinalis, who regularly came to see me in the mental hospital, had literally saved my life in New York a few months before.

So, I staggered down to the bar and said, "Jimmy, I've decided to do something about my drinking!" Jimmy meant it when he said, "Fantastic news, Ross." A half an hour later I was back saying, "For Christ's sake, give me a drink." That's how long I lasted, when I tried to stop drinking on my own - half an hour!

But instead of pouring me a drink, Jimmy handed me a phone number and said, "Get your arse out of here and ring this number." It turned out to be the number of Alcoholics Anonymous in Cleveland.

In fact, I've only been properly sober since I've been free of alcohol and all other drugs as well. Shortly after I went to an AA meeting in Cleveland, I got deported back home to Australia. The reason for my deportation is simple, and it still applies. If you're a non-resident in the state of Ohio and you make more than two notifiable suicide attempts, the authorities get very sick of paying the hospital bills. And they work out that it's much cheaper to pay your fare back to wherever you come from, Finland or in my case Melbourne.

The day before I left Cleveland in September 1969, I had rung *The Australian* newspaper, collect, to tell them this famous poet was coming home. The reality was I'd hardly written a note to the milkman, but as it eventuated on a Monday morning there was a big article, plus a photo, written about me, this sensitive poet with his hands trembling.

That afternoon, wearing an orange suit, a purple jerkin, and an Isadora Duncan scarf and armed with copies of *The Australian*, I went back to Her Majesty's Hotel to see some of my old teachers – to show them what a success I'd made of my life!

In those days, there was a secluded section of Maisies where a number of Melbourne High School teachers regularly drank after work. But before they arrived, I got back on the booze. After I king-hit one of the masters I cared about and respected, I ran out of the bar and headed to the Elwood home of a close friend of mine, Ken Gooding.

I had been to an AA meeting in Melbourne the night before and someone had given me a phone number. So Ken, who is my oldest friend, intervened and rang that number. It turned out that he'd called a sober member called Mick from Sandringham, who'd had a resentment against my father for years. This was because, in his first game playing for Carlton, my Dad was at the end of his career captaining Collingwood Seconds and in the first couple of minutes my dad whacked him in the head and said, "You're with the big boys now."

Mick took me to a meeting of Alcoholics Anonymous that night, in St Kilda. And there I met my Melbourne sponsor, Lee Parry who did something extraordinary; in all of our time together, he never criticised me once.

When we first met, Lee didn't know me from a bag of wheat. But he knew that my only chance of getting sober and staying on the planet was being taken to a whole lot of AA meetings. He took me and a German bloke every night for three months. The German bloke killed himself; he blew his head off with a double barrel shotgun.

After I tried to kill myself again by overdosing on tablets, I was admitted to an alcoholic and drug addiction hospital called Delmont. My friend Barry and I drank together and got sober together. Delmont was the last mental hospital either of us has been in as a patient. The night before we were due to be discharged, we got taken into a large AA meeting at the Malvern Town Hall. After the meeting I came up to a long-time member 'Antique Harry' in tears and said, "Do you ever think I'll get this thing, Harry?"

Instead of saying "No hope unless you get off the tablets," which is true but not very useful, Harry looked at me and said, with great gentleness; "Son, if you stay close to this movement, you will be alright." The fact is that I've got a large Adam's apple. Those words connected with my heart. But even then, I knew that Antique Harry couldn't have had faith in me. How could he? I was so damaged. Not just by all the alcohol and all the drugs I had consumed, but because I'd had loads and loads of shock therapy (ECT), in my case without anaesthesia.

I eventually came to realise that what Antique Harry had faith in was my regular attendance at AA meetings that start on time and finish on time, and, within that structure, sober members talk about they used to be like, what happened and what they are like now. This has done for me what all the money in a big city couldn't buy. AA has enabled me to not pick up the first drink of alcohol, one day at a time, and to lead a productive life.

I didn't get properly sober until I moved up to Sydney. It was Australia Day (January 26) 1970 that I threw away all the tablets I was taking. And since then, I've had nothing in my blood but blood. But the truth is if I hadn't stopped using as well as drinking at the age of twenty-five, I wouldn't have made twenty-six.

I attended AA meetings in Sydney every night for the first four years. Given my damaged mental state and parlous physical condition I didn't go to one too many. As the book *Alcoholics Anonymous* states, "A body that has been badly battered and a mind that has been badly burnt does not heal overnight." In my case, that was an understatement. Indeed, it took me three to five years in AA to get anywhere near emotionally and mentally together.

When I was a few decades sober in Brisbane, a Sorbonne-trained colleague at Griffith University, where I was Professor of History and Politics, put his nose in the air and said; "AA's just brainwashing." To which I replied, "It certainly is, and I've got the sort of brain that needs to be washed regularly."

The woman who'd lasted the longest with me in Cleveland was Rosemary. Towards the end of our relationship she fled to Akron, Ohio, where in 1935 Alcoholics Anonymous had begun. I wrote Rosie a pathetic suicide-note saying, "If anything should happen to me, please don't feel it's all your fault." Again, as someone who writes comedy, I now regard this as a very funny line, but the sad thing is that I meant it.

I'd met Rosemary in the week that I arrived in Cleveland. Our first date was a dinner, for which she paid. At the end of the swanky restaurant was a fortune-teller. And for the same reason that I'd (unsuccessfully) tried to join the Communist Party of Australia when I was sixteen and later went to India to study Zen and Hinduism, to try to find some meaning in my life, after our meal I consulted the fortune teller. Although I wasn't fall-down drunk, I'd been drinking quite a lot.

She first asked, "When were you born?" After I answered, "Christmas Day 1944", the fortune-teller said, "You must be a Capricorn" and I couldn't work out how she knew that. But then she told me things about myself that I thought no-one ever knew, including the fact that I felt like a garbage tip as a child, and that I had a mother who would lie when telling the truth would do. I listened to her intently, as these days I do to speakers at AA meetings. Then she said, "Ross, you are an alcoholic, and you will have to go to Alcoholics Anonymous." (This was almost two years before I first went to AA).

I was flabbergasted. When I asked, "How do you know I'm an alcoholic?" she said, "I can smell them a mile away." But when I asked, "How do you know I'll have to go to AA?" she looked at me straight between my eyes and said, "Because you will have nowhere else to go!"

I don't believe in fortune-telling, but it seems to me that this woman was almost certainly a member of AA or of Al-Anon (a fellowship which helps the relatives and friends of alcoholics) earning her living as a fortune-teller. Whatever the case, what she said to me is true. If I take my bat and ball and go home (which is what I once did as a narcissistic child), it's all over, red rover. In fact, AA is the only mob in which I've stayed where I haven't got my own way.

Even though I was fifty-two years sober on Australia Day (January 26), I still attend AA meetings two or three times a week. This is because if I stopped attending AA and doing what I need to do about the Twelve suggested Steps of recovery, the chances are highly likely that, sooner or later, I would drink again.

It is primarily at meetings of Alcoholics Anonymous, and especially at my Saturday 2:00 pm to 3:30 pm home group at South Sydney, where I am known as 'Redfern Ross', that I feel some sense of peace and serenity, and of usefulness. As I often say, "You don't have to like me, but I'm a remarkable example of how AA can transform a person, who was so damaged by booze and other drugs, into a functioning human being and a well-regarded historian, novelist and political commentator."

My beloved wife of 43 years, Lyndal Moor Fitzgerald, to whom my memoir *Fifty Years Sober: An Alcoholic's Journey* is dedicated, was 45 years sober when she died in January 2020.

Lyndal stopped drinking the first night we met at Sydney's St Vincent's Hospital AA meeting on Guy Fawkes Day (5 November) 1974. My first words to her were "If you only knew what could happen to you, if you stay close to AA." At the time, Lyndal would have fallen over backwards at the thought that we would become lovers a year later on Guy Fawkes Day (5 November) 1975, and that we would be married another year later, on Guy Fawkes Day (5 November) 1976.

While I'm also called 'Eight O'Clock Ross' (because I'm strong on meetings starting and finishing on time), Lyndal's AA nickname was 'Adequate from Arncliffe'. This was because, at her home group at Arncliffe which we attended together, she regularly talked about striving, in her work, for adequacy, not for perfection.

As a perfectionist, my rule pre-AA was "If at first you don't succeed, stop." But it was as a result of listening to Lyndal's wise words, coupled with paying attention to James Thurber's motto, "Don't get it right, get it written" that I started writing.

It was only after I met 'Adequate from Arncliffe' that I published my first book, a slim volume of poems, *The Eyes of Angels*, which was prefaced by this quotation: "Poets are damned but we are not blind, for we see with the eyes of angels." I've now authored or co-authored 43 books. This is in large part due to Lyndal's sage advice, and to her encouragement.

Shortly before she died on 22 January 2020, Lyndal said, "Do you know, Rossi, that in our 45 years together, you have never criticised me once."

I regard this as a great tribute to the AA movement. While I'm keen to continue writing fiction and non-fiction, now that darling Lyndal is dead, I need to remind myself, each day, that my primary purpose in life is to stay sober, and to help other alcoholics achieve sobriety.

> **Ross Fitzgerald AM** is Emeritus Professor of History and Politics at Griffith University. Professor Fitzgerald is the author or co-author of 43 books, most recently a memoir, *Fifty Years Sober: An Alcoholic's Journey*, and two Grafton Everest political satires co-authored with Ian McFadyen -*The Dizzying Heights* and *The Lowest Depths*, published by Hybrid in Melbourne.

2

Toni J

I remember the last twenty-four hours of active drinking. It was hell. I felt as though I was going to die. I was overwhelmed with fear.

I'd found the rooms of AA almost ten years earlier, but I really didn't want to stop drinking. I certainly didn't think that I was cut out for AA or that AA was the place for me. Yet, my drinking progressed and life became unbearable. I was so badly damaged and sick that I didn't even know it. But I did know something was wrong. I knew that I couldn't stop drinking and that I had to get professional help.

That morning I'd woken up looking for the morning drink to calm my nerves. I'd started drinking in the morning in the past few months because I couldn't stop shaking. My nerves were shot. I couldn't think straight. I was working, married, and bringing up two primary school aged kids. I was sick and tired of being sick and tired. I had had enough.

My head physically hurt. It felt as though something in my brain had shifted and although I had been reaching out to my then husband and family, no-one seemed to understand me. Maybe it was because I had never listened to them or taken notice of their concerns for many years previously. Still, I knew I was licked this time. I had nowhere else to go, but I didn't know that then.

I rang the hospital alcohol and drug service. I'd rung them several times over the past few years but never took action. This time, however, was different. They could see that I was desperate and told me to come into the hospital. I still wasn't sure that I'd go. I knew I had to, but I was so full of fear and arrogance that I didn't want to go. I didn't want to ask for help. I didn't want to admit defeat, yet I wasn't sure what I wanted.

I remember calling my father in the morning about 10:00 am. I told him I was trying to get help to stop drinking. I guess I was looking for sympathy, but instead all he could say was, "That's the best news I've heard all year!" I was complaining about a hole inside my chest. I felt like I was exposed, raw. It felt more like a hole in the soul, that I've since heard other members describe.

I struggled a lot growing up as a First Nations woman in Australia. I encountered a lot of racism. I'd had a successful life and career, but I always felt as though I didn't belong anywhere. I didn't feel comfortable in the rooms of AA because it was largely full of older non-Indigenous men and women. Still, I was so desperate that I didn't care anymore. I just needed to get well.

I'd had a few drinks – they were topping me up and eventually my ex-husband came home from work and drove me into the hospital. When we got to the hospital, I had a full assessment. I'd blown a high range blood alcohol reading. I didn't feel drunk, but I knew I wasn't sober. I stank of alcohol. I had extreme anxiety and couldn't sit still. By the time we had driven back home, the hospital rang me and advised that there was a bed available for me in the detox unit and that I needed to present to emergency first thing in the morning. I remember trying to pack a few clothes. I had very few personal belongings. At this stage I wasn't looking after myself very much. I had really let my appearance go and couldn't even look at myself in the mirror.

I remember going to bed that night. I'd had more to drink. I knew they would be my last couple of drinks. I went to bed praying, desperately calling out to God for help. I didn't know if I was going to make it through the night, I was so scared. I had no idea what I was doing and whether I would even get well. I didn't realise that I had surrendered at that point. All I wanted was to get out of the pain I was in, and I was prepared to do anything.

The next morning, I woke up early. I was in a state of fear. I just wanted to get to the hospital. My ex-husband had to drive me from the Gold Coast to Brisbane, about a fifty minute drive. I remember being so anxious and fearful. We didn't speak much. I felt as though I was in intense physical and mental pain. My head hurt and I felt the full force and weight of all my twenty-plus years of drinking alcoholically. It was confronting, daunting and nauseating – all at once.

By the time we got to the hospital, I was pacing the emergency ward. I couldn't sit still. I was finally called into a small waiting room to do a formal admission with one of the nurses. I can still remember the face of the nurse who I spoke to. She asked me a series of questions on a form using a clipboard. She didn't even look up at me. I assumed she must have seen so many people coming through the hospital before. She didn't seem impressed with me.

She asked me the usual questions and then she asked me if I had ever given up drinking before. I told her that I had stopped for three months several years ago when I had attended AA meetings. She stopped. She put her pen down and looked at me fairly and squarely in the eye. I'll never forget her next words. She said, "Don't you think that you should go back to AA?"

It was as simple as that. I had a moment of clarity. I saw in an instant that AA had worked and that I couldn't stop drinking without the help of a program like AA. Instead, I mumbled, "I guess so." Shortly afterwards I was taken to the alcohol and drug unit in the hospital. I was so scared. My husband left me, and I was told that I would be admitted for the next week without any visitors, no smokes, no phone contact and that I wasn't allowed to leave the hospital. I was so scared. I wanted to cry but I was overwhelmed with anxiety and pain. I remember being given valium and another medicine. I remember the kind faces on the staff inside the hospital ward. They were so patient and firm. I knew that I was broken and that I needed their professional help to get well. That was the second level of surrender that I had experienced in the last twenty-four hours.

I didn't sleep much that first night in hospital, but I felt safe. I liked the clean bed, the hospital sheets and food. It was the first time in a long time that I'd slept in clean sheets and eaten three healthy meals a day. By the third or fourth day, I was feeling so much better. It felt good to have a warm shower. We had to go to daily group activities. People from AA came into the hospital and spoke to us. I related to one of the women from AA who spoke to us. I knew I had to get to AA as soon as I was released from hospital. I had found a sense of hope and was now determined to give AA another go.

I have been coming to AA now for almost fourteen years, one day at a time, and my life has changed beyond recognition. Many of the promises of the program have come true for me. I live a full and richly rewarding life where I am able to help others and carry the message of recovery to newcomers. I have done so many things in recovery that I never thought would be possible. I have completed further university studies, set up my own business, and travelled overseas.

I have two adult daughters who I love deeply who have benefited immensely from my recovery. I will never forget the words of my daughters who said that the day I stopped drinking and found AA, was the day their lives began! Most of all, I have become the person that I believe God intended me to be from the outset. I've had to do a lot of inner work on myself, looking at my defects and making amends through the Twelve Steps.

I am exceptionally proud of who I am and even more proud of who I've become as a strong black woman who has walked this path and found a way out of darkness and fear. I have an incredible relationship with my Higher Power whom I call God. It is stronger than ever and the foundation of my life today. God does for me what I could never do for myself. Yet I must stay vigilant and useful, continually asking God for the strength, courage, and wisdom to face each day in God's love and light.

Toni is a First Nations woman and member of Alcoholics Anonymous. She grew up in north Queensland and later Canberra. Her family has ties to Cape York and the Torres Strait. She lives and works in Brisbane (Meanjin) and has two adult daughters. Toni is passionate about service in recovery and has been actively involved in compiling a book of personal stories of Indigenous members of AA. She is also a founding member of the National Indigenous Online AA meeting.

3

Tim Olson

I was brought up to witness that "The only recluse for an artist is intoxication." Oscar Wilde.

Well if it was good enough for an artist, then obviously it was good enough for me. For a long time, I believed that I was born a natural escape artist and probably had a propensity for drinking. I saw alcoholism as a disease I had carried from birth, a silent addict's gene. Many people think that it's something you develop gradually or adopt desperately during a hard time, a character defect or lack of willpower. By my early forties, I knew differently; I was in the claws of addiction, my drinking was an unmanageable crisis.

I cannot blame my addiction on my profession (as a gallerist and art dealer) but it certainly did not help. The art world eases you into a life where everything is bought, sold, resolved, and discussed over a shared bottle. My life was cushioned inside an illness that became more obvious as the drinks surfaced earlier each day. I was gradually becoming more and more detached from work and family, like a man living on a park bench within his own home.

Thank God I had wonderful staff at the gallery, because I was running the gallery from a distance. My business, in those great art-boom years, was expanding — and so was I. Drinking and eating far too much, I was literally fermenting and looked thirty years older. In summer, overweight and with a suntan, my mother would describe me as 'a map of self-indulgence'. I was treating my body like an amusement park. Few can see their most negative manifestations gradually engulfing them, but I would look in the mirror and could not recognise myself. Alcoholism (and obesity) was a mask that I could not remove. For those who have an innate fear of clowns, the face of Luna Park was perhaps less frightening than mine. It is terrifying when one becomes one's worst horror.

Every day was a quiet rampage. For most of the time, I was very good at getting through the day, but it was after everyone went to bed that I would reach into the back of a cupboard or look to the back of the fridge or freezer, and the bottle would open. I would sit, isolated, and I would drink myself into a morbid state of self-pity or oblivion.

My rock bottom was long overdue. I had been living in a state of delusion that I could get control over this thinking, that I was capable of being a controlled drinker. But ultimately, as life unfolded, it seemed evident that I was completely powerless over alcohol – anytime I started, I could not stop. I was living in a state of subconscious endlessness when it came to alcohol. The droll of daily anxiety, waiting for the early opener, or getting to a restaurant for lunch quickly.

In rehab, they talk about 'crossing the thin red line' from controlled drinking to problem drinking. I believe that trauma, (chronic business and personal stress, a car accident which left me in a coma as a child, my early childhood sexual abuse – and yes, my drinking habits and obesity) was my line.

One Christmas morning, after drinking all night, I found myself under the Christmas tree surrounded by empty bottles and yet-to-be-unwrapped gifts. My son, James, was three, and he was sobbing, pleading, "Daddy, Daddy, can you please help me open my presents?" Santa might have come and gone, but Dad was a mess on the floor. My head was feeling like it had been in a vice all night and my mouth was like the bottom of a cockie's cage. The alcoholic self totally pickled by the grog of the night before. Now my son was witnessing and becoming affected by my addiction. This was my precipice; "Enough was enough."

After somehow gathering myself together to attend the family Christmas lunch at my sister's, later that night I booked myself into the Betty Ford Centre in Palm Springs, and on Boxing Day was on the first flight to Los Angeles. I have seen alcoholism played out in both my grandfathers as emotional abuse and dependency. Remembering all of this, and the deep sense of shame and guilt, my greatest reason to stop was for James, to cease this cycle within the family chronology permanently.

One of the most alarming things that happened to me while I was completing my admission in Nevada desert, was being led into an office for my initial assessment to ascertain my state of addiction. There was a man, sitting behind a desk, who resembled Keith Richards. He had obviously been to hell and back and now he had assumed that calm mien of a wise sage of recovery. He asked me, "What is the worst thing that could happen to you if you left here and continued to drink?" Almost mechanically, I replied, "I'm going to die." It must have been what he had heard every time a new patient arrived, because he immediately replied, "No, that might not be the worst thing. Because, according to your family, you are a pain in the arse. They would be sad, of course, if you were to die, but ultimately they would be better off without you." I reeled with shock at the harshness of his words, but they turned out to be exactly the reality I needed to hear. Although originally only intending to stay at Betty Ford for a month, this extended to three. After thirty days I may have been sober but far from sane.

Betty Ford took an approach like no other rehab I had visited. Like a tattered tall ship, I had to have every sail ripped of grandiosity, denial and delusion torn down and dismantled so I could be rebuilt as a stronger vessel. I had to forget everything I thought I knew. I had to admit, and accept, that I was completely powerless over alcohol, to surrender and understand that I could not do this on my own, and to believe in the

prospect of a miracle in discovering a spiritual humility, to hand over my addiction to something that seemed invisible and intangible.

In rehab I was a nobody, just another addict. The Olsen name was not going to shield me or be advantageous, the buffer I had used as an excuse to be a bon vivant. Being isolated and anonymous on the other side of the world helped me focus on the delusion and ego I had been living in. A very big part of sobering up is realising that you are not special, that you are no better than anyone else. When you develop some kind of humility and go to meetings, with every kind of person, you realise that you are all reduced to being simply 'garden-variety' alcoholics, as they say. Alcoholism is very egalitarian. No one is immune. Often the privileged are its greatest victims.

I continued to attend AA meetings but I was not following the program and did not have a sponsor. My 'last drink' became my next relapse. A successful path to a truly happy life in sobriety requires a huge deflation in ego. To become brutally honest with oneself. It is a constant challenge when people keep praising your success when there is always a part inside you that feels like you do not deserve it. Another great quote of Oscar Wilde is "It is often worse to be destroyed by praise, than ruined by criticism."

The difference in coming back into the program was the realisation of the depth of my problem, the necessity for a sponsor and the dedication the program requires. I met Ross Fitzgerald at St. Mark's at Edgecliff, where my son went to Kindergarten. The last time I had been in that room, my James, was playing goldilocks – a blinding contrast. Now I go every morning to attend meetings at the Bondi Pavilion. In the 1930s, the Pavilion had a ballroom and a cabaret room where my grandparents attended parties and Harry, my grandfather, would drink to excess. The irony is not lost on me.

My commitment to battling alcoholism coincided with the spiky precipice that is turning fifty and the vulnerability to all that a midlife crisis implies. I then realised the pinnacle of sober living, "You cannot think your way into

a new way of living, you can only live your way into a new way of thinking." I could not think myself sober, only live myself into sobriety. It was not until I started putting days of avoiding alcohol together that abstinence became my lifestyle.

In the first weeks of going straight, I would use memory to trigger aversion. Memories of how squalid life had been with booze, waking up in the morning to reach into the freezer to take a swig of vodka, hanging out for the first pub to open, I had been an urbanised derelict.

When I eventually got completely sober, the clarity was both enlightening and frightening. Facing the truth of my past mistakes and behaviour was highly confronting. The only way to dissipate the shame was to accept it

as a learning experience, apologise and make amends where I could. Finally, I was able to make sense of things and realise how interesting and great my life had actually been.

I have now been sober for nearly eleven years. As I sit in my home, overlooking Sydney Harbour I know how lucky I am and that I would never have achieved any of this, and the success of my gallery (thirty years this year) if I had still been drinking. The gifts are apparent every day. AA is an invitation to live, to get a life !! As one may put it.

Getting sober was the best way for me to stop being a self-saboteur, an obstacle to my own happiness, and the happiness of those around me. Especially those that love me. For me, it was simple: I can have alcohol, or I can have everything. Thank God, I chose everything.

In technicolour.

> **Tim Olsen** is one of Australia's most recognised and respected art identities and successful gallery owners. Son of Australia's national living treasure, artist Dr John Olsen, A.O. O.B.E., Olsen was born into a life of modern and contemporary art. In 2020, Tim's memoir, Son of the Brush, was published by Allen & Unwin recounting his struggle

and recovery with addiction. The memoir has been awarded the 2021 Alex Buzo Shortlist Prize and the Nib People's Choice Prize for The Mark & Evette Moran Nib Literary Award.

4

Di Young

The last week of my last drink was preceded by an introduction to Alcoholics Anonymous. A man took me to AA for eight months although I continued to drink on and off and I was also a big narcotic user. I'm talking nearly forty-seven years ago now, so it was a very different time in society. Many people with narcotic addictions didn't survive and I walked away from AA thinking I was different. I was very young, and in retrospect, I was quite damaged not only from my alcoholism and drug taking, but also from my childhood. So I left Alcoholics Anonymous with a 'flick of the then, long blonde hair,' and in my inimitable fashion, stole a car and drove up the coast as we did in those days, "In the spirit of freedom."

I often suffered quite long blackouts when I drank. A blackout, as I understand it, is where people still function and talk and do things but for all intents and purposes have no recollection of it when they come out of it. The last blackout lasted three or four days and when I came to I was in a little place called Wooli, on the North Coast. I was mid-sentence talking to somebody I'd known from Sydney in a room with a fire in the middle, and immediately did a quick double take. I was pretty quick on my feet even though I was battered around by this disease. I thought to myself, "What am I talking about to you? Who are these other people? Where am I actually?" All along trying to not let anyone know that I had absolutely no clue where I was or what I was doing there. I quickly had to piece it together. It was probably over a period of the next hour, I worked out where I was, what day it was, and how many days I'd lost in the blackout.

It became obvious to me that my saving grace was that I'd seen people who had recovered. And whilst I didn't think I was one of them at that time, when I came out of that blackout I realised I had a problem that was more serious than I previously thought. That felt like an understatement, isn't it significantly serious when you lose four days of your life? I looked outside to the stolen car and knew I had to get help. I managed to tidy myself up, get back in the car and back to Sydney. From that point onwards I started to get well.

I had been raised by an alcoholic mother and a father who drank just as much but was not an alcoholic, he was a chronic gambler. From the age of sixteen I was on the streets and to be honest, I was young and reasonably good looking so I could always find some unsuspecting person to find me somewhere to stay. There were a bunch of people out there doing the same thing and I ended up belonging to a sort of quasi community, if I can call it that, where people looked out for each other.

It became obvious to me that I needed help, but I was on the streets. I met a man who was thirty years older than me, he was a career criminal. To be perfectly honest, I wasn't going to listen to anyone who wasn't a little bit bent. If a good Christian said to me "I can save you," I would have run a mile, but I'd listen to somebody left of centre. I got together with this man and onto the next part of my criminal career.

It was back in the days when there was fast money in manipulating poker machines and my job was to put the money in a fashionably large handbag and carry it out the door. I became hooked on this activity. I thought the biggest problem I had was a lack of money and that this man was the best thing I'd found in a long time.

He took me to my first AA meeting and I went with him for the next eight months. I wasn't sober all of that time. I didn't really know what anyone was talking about and thought "It was all very well for those people." I was eighteen years old and didn't consider myself burnt out, although in many ways I was. I was six and a half stone, I had scabies, hair right down my back, and didn't know the last time I showered. I wasn't page three in Vogue that's for sure. After eight months of being taken to meetings I found the courage to say to him "I don't want to go anymore" because alcohol had rendered me mute. Then of course, I stole that car, went to the North Coast and came out of the blackout.

I don't think I was particularly frightened of dying, what I was tired of were the rehearsals, that dreadful going on and on and on. Not wanting 'it' to happen again and then 'it' happening again, and knowing that I had no power over anything in my life. Alcoholism is a lonely disease and I had been alone and lonely for a very long time. I didn't look like it, but my soul was full of despair because of how my life was.

I had eight months of exposure to people who were like me, even though in many respects they were very different to me, and trying to get well. They spoke the language of recovery and that there was a way out of this. When I finally came back to the meetings after that bust I thought "Ok, I'll try and do it AA's way not my way and see what happens." I had no desire to go back out again.

Whilst my drinking wasn't that long compared to many people's drinking, the wreckage of it took a good while to tidy up. The police did eventually catch me. I was sort of hiding out in a caravan in Narrabeen and trying to stay sober and work out what the hell to do with my life.

Now this is not the last week of my drinking but It speaks to the madness I lived with. We got arrested just before I got sober and it took two years for the trial to come up. I went to jail when I was two years sober. The three men involved all went to prison. I had barrister's fees to pay and no money so I got a job as a shorthand typist but it was a joke. I forgot how to do shorthand and I certainly couldn't type so I fudged it, I was good at that. It was at a conservative insurance company and a time when women had to wear dresses so I borrowed a few frocks from AA women.

I told a few fibs to get the job and then after a couple of weeks, the gentleman who had employed me stayed back one night. I thought he was going to sack me. He said, "How are we going?" I said, "We're not going very well are we?" He said "No, we're not. What seems to be the problem?" I said "I told a whole lot of lies to get this job. I realise I can't do it. I'm actually in AA and I've had an alcohol and drug problem." He asked "What drugs have you been using?" I said "I've been using heroin." Then he asked "How often do you go to meetings?" I said, "Well, I go every day, sometimes twice on Saturdays and Sundays," and I did.

He asked "Would you go back to night school and learn to do what I'm paying you to do?" "Yes," I replied. He said "Hang on a second, how would you get to the meetings every night? What happens if you don't get to them?" "I would drink, I guess, if I don't go." He said "Forget about the night classes, I'll teach you what you're supposed to know." So he dictated, "Dear Mr Smith" and I was writing longhand, then I'd go out and type it up.

Two years passed and I worked hard. I wanted to turn my life around. I went into his office and said "Mr Perkins, can I talk to you with the door shut?" The door was never shut, which meant this was serious. "There's a part of my story I didn't tell you, I need to resign." When he asked why I told him "I'm going to jail." "You're going to do what?" I told him about my upcoming court-case and he said, "Leave it with me" and discussed it with his boss. They said to put in for annual leave.

We were all found guilty and it was splashed over the newspapers. I went to jail for two weeks and there was no illusion of what we had been doing. The irony was that as I was leaving to go on annual leave, the women I worked with asked, "Will you be staying in Sydney for your holidays darling?" "Yeah," I'm thinking, "I'll be at Silverwater prison." The judge found us guilty and said "I'm sending you all back to jail for the weekend and will sentence you Monday. The three men had character witnesses to speak for them and I had nobody, I thought, "Why didn't anybody tell me about this? On Monday they called out Mr Thompson who was Mr Perkins' boss, and he spoke for me. "She's worked for us in the insurance company for two years and she's never had a day off." The judge asked Mr Thompson directly "If I let her out of jail, does she have a job with your firm?" and he said "Yes, absolutely."

I was released because of that and had to report weekly for five years. The judge said "If you don't turn up one week, a warrant will be issued for your arrest and you will serve five years." I didn't miss one week I can assure you. Those two men who took a chance on me, and their kindness, is an extraordinary part of my story. I kept working for them for a good while before I changed careers. There's great value in being given a second chance, and a third.

My story is a mixture of having dipped into recovery and relapsing big time. I knew the difference because I had heard people at AA meetings talk about changing their lives, and I thought if I do as they do I too might have a chance.

> Di is a Trauma-informed therapist, Systemic and Family Constellation practitioner with significant experience mentoring and working with people and families affected by addiction.

5

Sally M

My name is Sally M and I'm alcoholic.

The wheels had been coming off for a couple of years. I didn't know I had an alcohol problem and I didn't know what alcoholism was. It was like I was blinkered and deaf to that narrative. I worked with a Director on a film who said to me "I'm in AA" and all I said was "Alright, what's on today" and glossed over it.

There was another friend who I knocked about with as kids and she was mad and crazy and definitely always drunk. She ended up as my Real Estate agent and looked amazing, on top of the world, and I said "What's happened to you? You look incredible." She said "I went to AA. I don't drink" and I said "Oh interesting. Who's renting my house?"

I liked those two people and many years later when the opportunity came, I had no resistance going to AA because they had mentioned it. I don't remember hearing about AA anywhere else. My Grandfather was an alcoholic but I didn't drink like him. I didn't think I drank like alcoholic people. I thought alcoholics were men with paperbags in the park or like my Grandfather and that was not me.

My last drink was in 2007 and I was thirty-seven. I had a pretty successful year on paper and in my external world I looked successful. I had a couple of films, had been overseas to Berlin and Cannes film festivals and walked up the red carpet but always ended up drunk at the after parties.

I had a great job and I was going alright but there was nothing I liked about any part of my life, and I had never hated myself as much. I was drinking in a way that was worrying me because I couldn't seem to not drink. I was drinking things I would never drink, like rum and coke. I didn't like rum and I didn't like coke and I was buying these cans and drinking a case at night and waking up face planted into the ground in my lounge room. Waking up just before my daughter woke up for school. And I was so messy, I had two bedrooms on the run so when I got really messy I could just change to another room. I had taken to buying two pairs of shoes because I often lost a shoe when I went out. But the worst thing was I always lost the same shoe, same foot. So I always had all these 'one' shoes.

I was going slowly mad and there was one night the drink was not working. Sometimes it would work and sometimes it didn't. One night when it didn't work and really disturbed me I went and put myself in a laundry dryer, in one of those big public 24 hour laundromat dryers. I was so drunk I couldn't close the door to turn it on. I thought "That's a great way to go while my daughter is asleep at home, it will look like an accident."

I decided to go to Sydney and clean myself up. That's how I was going to put a cork in the bottle. My daughter must have been with her father for the school holidays.

I was looking after my stepmother's posh apartment in Potts Point. I invited friends for a dinner party, a lovely view, and to show them some films that had won awards. I made this film which was as good as I had done, and it had a profound effect on me and I wanted to show it to my friends. The film centred on an Aboriginal survivor of a massacre by white landowners.

One of the crazy things in my drinking is that I would hear clap sticks, and I lived close to Kurilpa Park in Brisbane, a strong and important Aboriginal stronghold. At the time I made the film, our family's Aboriginal history had not been confirmed. I had been agitating, "Are we or aren't we Aboriginal? I always wondered,

"Was my grandmother from the stolen generation?" My Aunty and I couldn't find any information at that stage.

Back at the dinner party to show that film; I had the table set, white tablecloth, lovely glasses. I told guests "I'm not drinking so bring your own drinks, please bring your own drinks, I'm not drinking." I made a real song and dance about it.

About 5.30pm I was organised. I wasn't drinking. I was edgy, that edge, and I thought "I'll just have a drop, a lick. I won't have a full glass, not even a sip, just a lick of wine, a drop, to take the edge off."

And I opened the cork and the genie was out of the bottle again. I was off and running, drinking everyone's wine at dinner. I cracked open my stepmum's wine cabinet. I don't remember what I did or didn't do, half the people went home after the meal and the other half went to a club in Kings Cross, then another club, and another. It was no different to any other time I drank. It was drinking and chaos like any other night I went out since I was fifteen. It was the last 'man' standing kind of thing.

My friend and I were not allowed into another club around 4:00 or 5:00 am but we knew the bouncer and got taken around to the back door. And as we go in she trips over and lands head first across the floor and hits a brass rail and I see her do that and think "I'm going to pretend I didn't see that and I'm going to order myself a couple of vodka and tonics because I can drink hers as well." I didn't go and see her. I was just focused on getting four quick hits of vodka as fast as I could. Then she came up and said "Did you see what happened?" and I said "No, I didn't and I bought you a drink but I drank it."

I was disgusted with my own behaviour. I have an awful memory of trying to throw myself over the balcony but I was too drunk to do it. I thought it would look like an accident. I couldn't lift myself up over the railing, I was too inebriated. Worst thing was I was still as edgy as I was at that first lick.

I'd been drinking for fourteen hours and it hadn't touched the sides, the madness was still with me.

That's what flicked the switch for me. When I got everyone up and got them out I went downstairs and to my horror there was a note on very nice embossed paper saying "We do not tolerate the kind of behaviour we have seen on the security cameras. This is cause for total eviction."

I don't remember what we all did but this was cause for eviction. It was my stepmother's home, so these combinations of things were shameful. What really got to me though was the alcohol hadn't worked. I traced it back to the first lick. How had it happened that I was only going to have a lick and fourteen hours later I was in this place?

All that behaviour went down and I wasn't even drunk and I was terrified. I knew and I said these words out loud to myself "The game is up! I can't drink and I can't not drink. If there is help, can help please come?"

I was so crook, I was as crook as a person would be crook given the amount I drank. For the next twenty-four hours I thought I was dying. I carried on like a pork chop. I went to the doctors and had blood tests done and my liver function was perfectly fine. We have livers like Phar Lap's heart in my family.

I was furious. I went home and I rang my friend who I'd been out with and said "I'm sick, I don't know what's wrong." She said "I'm going to support my cousin at an Alcoholic Anonymous meeting tonight in Bondi." And without flinching I said, "I think I will come and support your cousin too." I didn't know her. Never met her, and I went to the meeting and I heard two people share. I recall they said they didn't have a drink at their father's funeral, and I thought "What a pair of liars, you can't go to a wake and not drink" and it perplexed me.

When we left the meeting my friend said "Those people are mad" and I hadn't thought that. I thought "They are telling the truth and I'm confused but if I need to drink I might go back there, but I think I will be alright."

And two weeks later I went home to Brisbane. l stayed off the drink, but I was then seven days into withdrawals. I was seeing dead people floating in the river. I had electric fleas. I couldn't count money. My mind didn't work as alcohol was the absolute glue to my existence and without it my brain was mush and marshmallow.

It was Friday afternoon and I went to a cafe for a coffee and I thought I would drink but didn't want to, and I was terrified. I realised that I could have been dead and I thought "If I drink, my daughter would be an orphan" and I didn't want to but thought I would drink. Earlier that morning I watched an episode of Oprah and an actress said "I want to do better." She woke up and knew she could do better and left her husband and I thought, "I want to do better."

I was thinking "I'm going to drink" and then "I just can't do it." And in the corner of the cafe was a stack of telephone directories. A stack of A to K's. And I just saw A,A,A,A,A,A. I kept looking at A,A,A,A.

I remembered a film 'The Day of Wine and Roses' where the man opens the phone book and sees the AA number and I thought "It won't be there," but I opened it and there was the number. I rang the number and they suggested going to a meeting that night in Nundah and my arrogance kicked in and I said "I can't go there." They said "Beenleigh?" and I said "I would never go there," "Coorparoo?" and I said "No, I don't know who you think I am." They said "You need a meeting or you will drink. What about Bulimba?" and I said "I love Bulimba. There's a cinema there, I'll go there."

And l went and it was a library and I didn't see the banners. I saw a man with nice shoes and another in a Zelda suit and I thought "I might marry him" and someone shook my hand and offered me a seat. No one had welcomed me in that way for a very long time, and they stood up and talked about the madness and not needing to drink, and I identified with being mad and wanting to drink. I could see that they weren't mad and I identified with them and I realised I was not alone and that with them I might have a chance. Two women took me aside and told me where the next meeting was and I just jumped on the gravy train as I saw it.

I haven't had a drink from that day to this, over fifteen years.

In the first year of my sobriety, my Dad's cousin found out we are descendants from a Wiradjuri woman, a sole survivor of a massacre, and I was later confirmed by an elder in Wellington, and Mudgee. My Mum died of cancer early in my sobriety too, and painted a vase with a kookaburra, because I always had an affinity with them, like a totem for me, and after Mum passed, I found out the word kookaburra is a loan Wiradjuri word *Guggaburra*. An enormous amount of spirituality has come into my life since sobriety. I continue to feel guided by a connection to all my ancestors and now am most at home on Wiradjuri Country.

> **Sally M** is a producer and enjoys offering mentorship that champions visibility and emotional empowerment for women.

6

Richard Whitaker

Looking back – I'd been drinking heavily for many years before I realised that I had a tiger by the tail. If I let go the tiger would eat me, if I didn't he would also eat me, perhaps a little more slowly.

I think I started drinking alcoholically at around the age of twenty-four. Three years before I was a National Serviceman and I did two years in the Army from 1969 to 1970 where it was very much a drinking culture. It wasn't regarded as poor form to get drunk, as long as you were on parade the next morning and did your job, no problems. For the most part this did me no great harm, however, with my addictive personality, it did not end well. I've since learned that the modern Army does a great deal to assist personnel with this issue, but fifty years back that wasn't the case.

After I left the Army I joined the Public Service and frequently drank heavily by myself at night, and it was euphoric. Drinking was particularly magical in the early days but the problem was as I became increasingly resistant to alcohol I had to drink more and more to achieve the same impact. That was my tiger, and I dared not let go, no matter how much I wanted to.

I had tried to give up several times, always inventing new ways of cutting down rather than giving up and also using various low alcohol drinks to fool myself that I was making progress. I thought I could safely have one a day, perhaps two, or maybe only on the weekend. Without knowing it I was experimenting with controlled drinking, but for my brand of alcoholism there was no control.

I once went dry for six weeks but eventually drifted back to the normal pattern of drinking every night, mostly by myself, and waking the next day to the usual hangover and fears of what I might have said to my family, on the telephone, or to any guests that might have arrived unexpectedly. I didn't like having guests, thinking they might get the wrong impression, or in reality the right one.

My drinking was progressively impacting my life, home, and work, although I always found ways of convincing myself that nobody knew of my dark secret. My wife and family certainly did, but I found ways of excusing my conduct, and thereby avoided responsibility.

Strangely, I had been an athlete for many years before, religiously running a set course of seven kilometres every day, and achieving a high level of fitness. That was considerably blunted though by my large alcohol intake after I had returned home from my run. I had always placed great store on physical fitness and certainly managed to achieve this, but then largely undid it with alcohol, as with many other facets of my life. Alcohol was steering my life in precisely the opposite direction to where I wanted to go.

I read lots of articles about what the definition of an alcoholic was, but always found a way of excusing myself from all the various definitions "I was nothing like the derelict in the park with a brown paper bag, I had far more control over my drinking than that, didn't I?"

My drinking continued to escalate, I progressed from beer to white wine, always having to drink more and more to achieve the same buzz but never quite getting there. I became convinced that my set of problems was unique and I had just got to learn to live with them.

That last week of drinking I had a particularly bad period of binge drinking and I woke up one morning with an appalling hangover and thought the time had come. I just couldn't do this any more. My life would go completely down the gurgler from this point unless I stopped drinking alcohol. So, that was my position coming into the last week of my drinking.

The thought of not drinking was absolutely frightening. "How would I sleep? What would I do in the evenings? What if I couldn't handle it and went back on the grog? It may be entirely impossible for me to give up, in which case I'm doomed." I thought I was very much by myself at this stage and was facing a set of problems unique to me.

Many years before I remembered seeing a black and white Ray Milland film 'The Lost Weekend' about a man's descent into total alcoholic disaster, including delirium tremens, across a weekend of terror during which he totally lost his soul to the bottle. I saw this film as a boy and I was very interested in it. All the drunks I had seen in previous films were depicted as humorous characters with red noses often falling over in the street with everybody laughing about it. But as I was progressively finding out it was no laughing matter. 'The Lost Weekend' was the first time I saw drunkenness and alcoholism depicted in a real sense with the absolute degradation of the human spirit. I could see myself walking this road and the possibility filled me with horror and disgust.

The solution to this deadly predicament came through an entirely unexpected source. One night, in my usual drunken stupor, I did a Google search and purely by chance found a book called 'My Name Is Ross' about a man who had successfully used Alcoholics Anonymous (AA) in his battle with alcohol. I ordered the book online and it arrived a few days later. I read it cover-to-cover in forty-eight hours. The first thing that struck me was that many of the issues the author Ross Fitzgerald mentioned were very similar to those I was concerned with, and for me this was instant relief. It meant that I was not alone, one of my greatest fears.

I had known about AA through films and newspaper articles but hadn't sought it out. At that stage I thought AA was a bunch of religious zealots who prayed to God for their salvation. As an atheist this concept was unappealing, but it was also totally untrue as I was to discover.

I looked Ross up on the Internet, got a phone number, called him up and explained my situation and he invited me to an AA meeting. I said "Gosh I'm not that bad." He knew that was complete nonsense, but he guessed that I wasn't ready. His first advice, "Don't drink today and come to a meeting."

I sat on it for about three weeks and phoned him again and said "I've had second thoughts about your offer." He was in South Sydney so a drive across town was necessary. He gave me the AA meeting time and place and I met him outside the location at 1:30 pm on a Saturday. That was three weeks after I read his book.

That first meeting was an absolute revelation to me because I didn't know anything about AA, and I didn't know the concept of sharing as used at an AA Meeting. That day the members were from all walks of life. They included a university professor, a judge, a labourer, a bus driver and two men who had been to gaol, as diverse a group you would ever meet. I was to understand later that alcoholism knows no social boundaries.

I learned the structure of an AA meeting as they shared their experience of alcohol. They talked about "What it was like then, what it's like now and what happened in between." Several had minimal education but were articulate and wonderfully descriptive in outlining their lives as prisoners of alcohol.

All this reinforced my newfound belief that I was not unique at all. I heard about the common symptoms and consequences of alcohol addiction that these people had experienced, and in fact, I was going through just the same process. My rehabilitation as a human being had begun. I diarised my early recovery. I called it 'The Diary of a Recovering Alcoholic'. I kept records of my feelings for the first year. They became less detailed as the year went on but I felt it important to get them written down before I forgot them. I recorded my rediscovery of me, the rebirth of personal dignity and the slow evaporation of my agitation and irrational fears that had always been part of my psyche, but greatly amplified by alcohol.

In June 2022 I achieved ten years of sobriety, a real milestone. I don't regard myself as cured at all, but I do regard myself as being in remission. Since being in AA I've met several people who haven't drunk for many years but I also met a chap recently who picked up after being sober for seventeen years. That showed me that for many, including myself, alcoholism is an incurable disease.

There is no chance that I could have stopped drinking of my own accord, for me the desire to drink was, and possibly still is, more powerful than my desire to stop. But with AA in my corner, and powered with the combined wisdom of many who have been able to achieve sobriety, I have discovered, indeed proved, that it is possible to stop drinking.

I now believe that alcohol is by far the most destructive drug in our society, causing untold tragedy to individuals and families. Alcohol addiction fills our mental hospitals, trauma units, gaols, and road accident wards. The financial costs to be borne by the taxpayer are immense. For now I have beaten the tiger but I know he is still out there, watching and waiting for me to stumble.

> **Richard Whitaker** is a meteorologist and author of several publications, mostly about history and the weather. A recent book "Australia's Natural Disasters" (New Holland) went into a second edition in 2021. He is also a mathematician with several published papers to his credit.

7

Steve T

Since leaving school I have always worked. I started out as an apprentice mechanic at a local car dealership when I was sixteen years old. I was drinking at lunch with my older colleagues. I wanted to do more with my life so at seventeen I joined the army and became a soldier. After leaving the military I joined the emergency services and became a first responder. I have worked in this industry for the last thirty-three years.

I started drinking from an extremely young age and by the time I reached the legal age to drink I was quite a seasoned drinker. I was getting drunk when I was thirteen or fourteen years old and by the time I was about fifteen I was drinking alcoholically, getting so drunk I couldn't walk or talk properly. When I was sixteen, I was drinking in pubs and nightclubs. There weren't the strict enforced legal requirements to show proof of age back then. Drinking alcohol was like an escape for me.

I was a self-conscious kid who grew up in the suburbs of Adelaide, South Australia where the kids I hung out with were a little older. I was always the smaller, quieter one. I always knew I was different from my mates when I drank. I was always in a hurry to get as much alcohol in me as possible so I could feel that confidence alcohol gave me. That loss of inhibition where I felt ten feet tall and bulletproof. I remember in the early years of my drinking, alcohol gave me a kind of bravado and made me more of an extrovert as opposed to the introvert I felt I was when I was sober.

If I was drinking in a round with others, I used to sneak extra pints in when I went up to the bar to get my shout. I used to get quite annoyed and embarrassed when people criticised and commented on my excessive drinking. I saw it as a weakness if I couldn't handle my drink.

On occasions I would fool myself into thinking I could control my drinking. To prevent myself getting extremely drunk I would start the night by drinking low alcohol beer and go out with the intention of drinking water in between alcoholic drinks. I would also tell myself not to mix different types of alcohol, however, once I started to get drunk all bets were off and I drank as much alcohol as I could. I didn't care if it was beer, red wine or spirits.

In 1999, after a relationship breakup I tried to stop drinking. I managed to white knuckle it for ten months which was a real struggle for me. I didn't know anything about alcoholism, and after a long break I still thought I could control my drinking. My first drink back after this ten month break was the same as my alcoholic drinking prior. I went straight back to drinking until blackout. I had driven my car that night as I went out with every intention of not drinking. I parked my car in a multi-level carpark in the city and I remember waking up drunk in the front seat of my car. Fortunately, I hadn't driven, but I had wet myself and the sheepskin seat covers in my car were all soaked with my urine.

I was thirty years old and still living like I was when I was eighteen. I was getting too old for the night club scene but when I had a drink that didn't seem to matter to me. The ten month break of alcohol meant nothing once I was back on it. I was back to being that guy who just got shitfaced whenever I had a drink.

I continued to drink alcoholically for another three years after that and I was thirty-three years old when I had my last drink. My last twenty-four hours of drinking was 'The Big Day Out' music festival on the Gold Coast. I remember it was on a Sunday, however, I can't remember too many of the bands who were playing as I was pissed when I got there. I had been out the night before. When I woke up on Sunday morning, I was already half cut so I only needed a few drinks to feel fully charged again. It was an extremely hot January day, and I had a big sombrero hat on. I was bright red, and burnt as I was outside drinking all day.

My last day of drinking wasn't my worst day on the drink as far as behaviour was concerned, however, my mental state was at breaking point. Nothing too bad had happened on this last day other than I had been a bit of a nuisance to my first responder colleagues whom I knew who were working at the festival. I didn't get into trouble or insult anyone, but I had embarrassed myself. I suffered periods of blackout and there are long periods of this day that I cannot remember.

I do remember that I ran into a friend who I knew was a member of AA. I worked with this person, and he obviously identified me as an alcoholic long before I was prepared to accept this fact. He used to say things like "Your name's on a chair" but I didn't really understand what he was talking about. When he used to ask me about my drinking, I always felt extremely uncomfortable and wanted to change the subject. He obviously said enough to me as it was he who I sought out when I wanted to give up drinking.

I knew I had to stop drinking as my blackouts were getting worse. I would often wake up with bruising and swelling to parts of my body that I couldn't explain. I was getting into fights when I was drinking, and this was causing trouble at work. I had no money. My relationships were a disaster, and my mental and physical health was starting to deteriorate. I had been thinking about trying to stop for a long time prior and when I actually 'sobered up' after my last drink I reached out to my friend who was a member of AA. I believe it was fate that I saw this person on the last day of my drinking.

I went to this member's home on the Wednesday night after my last drink. I spent Monday and Tuesday sobering up, and usually by Wednesday I was ready to have another big drink. I can't remember the exact conversation I had with the member, however, he gave me his copy of the 'Big Book' and told me to just read the stories at the back to see if I identified with them. I identified with every story.

On Saturday night the AA member picked me up and I went to my first AA meeting. I remember feeling like a big weight was lifted off my shoulders as I was doing something positive about my drinking. I was single at the time and wasn't involved in a relationship so I could concentrate entirely on myself. I had been in relationships prior, and my drinking always caused dramas. I wasn't violent, however, I was unreliable. I was not a good partner. It always got too much for the other partner and I wanted to push them away so I could just drink the way I wanted to drink.

Since getting sober my whole life has changed. I have been sober for twenty years now. I have a job that I have been in for thirty-two years. When I was drinking I was a day to day proposition and it would have only been a matter of time until my employer had shown me the door. In the state that I was in I would have been unemployable.

Today I have a senior position within my organisation. I am married to a beautiful woman who is supportive in many ways and helps me live a sober life. We have five incredible children who are my whole world. I still have difficult days and I have to work hard at maintaining my sobriety.

AA meetings are essential for me and remind me of where I have come from and what is awaiting me if I decide to drink again. All that I have achieved in my twenty years of sobriety will disappear if I drink again. They say that the only requirement for AA membership is a desire to stop drinking. My desire today is stronger than when I first gave up drinking as I have far more to lose.

> **Steve T** is a father of five and employed as a police officer. He is currently completing a Bachelor of Fine Arts in painting and is interested in art history.

8

Shane

In the last week of my drinking I was unemployed and unemployable, and living from day to day. I was drinking sporadically and still drinking with a hope that alcohol would work for me the way it used to work for me.

Towards the last week of my drinking when I picked up a drink I found I would quickly enter into a state of being stupefied by alcohol and be unable to really interact with people around me. I found myself drinking on my own and in isolation and inevitably ending up in a drunken stupor very quickly. In the event that I was with other people I would often enter into a blackout and I could wake up having done anything.

Towards the very end, it was just a frustration and I was unable to beat the game or make alcohol work for me the way it once did. Alcohol just always had its way with me. I was living in a country town on the NSW coast called Woolgoolga. I didn't have any friends left at all, only the occasional person that I would run into. In my case I was smoking drugs during the day and drinking during the night.

That last week, I think I was just walking around as a lost soul, a lost person, and I had to drink with this disappointment, and frustration, and bewilderment at what had become of me, and why I couldn't manage alcohol. And why it was so dramatically managing me, my disposition and my ability to relate to everyone else.

Those last few drinks seemed to really isolate me as a human being from the rest of the human race. I am aware of this now in hindsight but at the time, obviously my mind and my soul was just full of a bewildering confusion at the state I was in, and how alcohol failed to work for me. It brought with it more chaos, more destruction, and chipped away at my enthusiasm for life. It plummeted me further and further into a lower state of being. This huge depression would descend on me and when I sobered up I had this terrible anxiety that the irreparable was about to occur. There was a great sense of impending doom that was surrounding me as well.

Having grown up in an alcoholic family and seen the wreckage of alcoholism all around me, I feared the absolute worst. There was a real sense of becoming quite desperate, fearing that I felt so lonely and in the event of a blackout I would suicide or hurt someone else. That was my state of mind and how out of control I'd become.

One of my last drinks, I went around to a person's house and I sat with three or four of my other peers and they were trying to talk to me and I thought I was talking back to them in a lucid, legible way, but they just looked at me with their faces sort of screwed up as if to say "We can't understand anything you're saying." I'm looking out from this being and I'm just completely confused again. My body was drunk but my mind was still almost sober. This is after repetitively trying to get alcohol to do something that it once did for me.

And even though I was young, I knew that it would forever be that way, because of the number of failures I'd had, endeavouring to get it to work the way it once did. It was almost like I was confronted with the fact that there was no going back to the good old days. I was aware that that pattern was real and that pattern would never change. I can't explain why I had that experience at that age which has consequently given me the experience I've had with AA for the last thirty-four years.

Then there was a friend of the family stepping into my world from time to time to have a talk with me. He had been in that world I was living in, he'd been a bikie from the Coffin Cheaters in Melbourne. I was quite impressed with his gangster approach to things, I would think "Mate, you are so cool." That was my perception of him. But he was sober and telling people around town that he was in AA, like a bit of a preacher. So, then I started to sort of almost hang out with him, he befriended me. My friends started to think that I was ready to turn my back on them and turn in a different direction. Which was his influence on my life, he encouraged me to do that.

Slowly I saw that my peers, who were drinking as I was drinking, weren't as badly affected by alcohol like I was. I looked at them and thought "What have these people got to offer me?" and I looked at him and thought "Perhaps, he has a way out of this mess that I find myself in."

The crunch came and I moved out of the house that I was in and moved back home. I thought, "I'm going to do something about my drinking." The very next day, the police went around to that house and kicked the doors in and they were dressed in their padded vests and had guns, and searched for drugs and lined everyone up and searched them. This was a warning to me. I had a bit of a rocky start because I was going to AA meetings and going home and smoking dope and philosophising about AA. He was also hooked up with a religious guy who was interpreting revelations. We were talking about the end of the world and the number of the beast and this sort of stuff.

There was part of me that was really looking for something else. Looking for something to give a bit of purpose to my life and a bit of meaning and direction, which I had none of while I was in the midst of practising alcoholism. I moved back home and started going to AA meetings and I then started meeting other people who were in the program. I did that for about six months and I got a job up towards Grafton at a blueberry farm. I was full of anxiety and fear and I was a wreck of a person. I couldn't cope with the reality of life, finding it hard to turn up to work and discipline myself and communicate with people and I thought "This is not going to work for me."

I ended up in a long term program in William Booth institute. This gave me distance between my last drink and drug and I was on my way. There's a whole period over the last twelve months of my drinking, rather than the last week where it was all a bit rocky and all over the place, a bit like experimenting, as the Big Book puts it.

Seeing if I could get away with it, not wanting to face the facts, and that resistance which comes into play.

Around this time in my life I was getting these weird creepy dreams. I would wake up with the terrors in the middle of the night. I heard a voice saying "if you keep doing what you're doing, you're going to end up in the gutter with a pick hanging out of your arm." And I could see the image. And that voice came through the dream like a booming megaphone, like it was a voice with authority and power. In my dream it was a voice outside of me. I understand that sensation. Not that it wasn't coming from a direction. It was just outside and all around me. I was starting to hallucinate and hear things as well. I started hearing trumpets in the car one day, like it was the end of the world, and I was like on the verge of a psychotic breakdown. I was becoming a religious psychotic. I was mixing pot and faith, and when you start predicting the future then you think you're a prophet or something.

Eventually, I surrendered and I was really at the point where I made a decision to make the William Booth institute program work for me. There was another person who came along who had been through the William Booth program, and I was impressed by the way he spoke about the institute.

So it's hard to put this in the last week, it's not necessarily straightforward. And the way I speak about it at the meetings, people think that I just woke up one day and stopped drinking and came to AA and had a smooth journey because I usually don't give all the details.

> Country town drunk to retired businessman, hopes and dreams fulfilled. **Shane** is thirty-four years sober, coming up to thirty-five in November this year.

9

Clare W

My last drink was actually warm, white wine from a cask, I think it may have been Mozelle. It was at a friend's home. It was his mother's wine and she kept it under the sink for cooking. It was the only alcohol left in the house. What had happened was I was working in a Golf Club, I felt like my career had kind of gone backwards. I started off years ago studying landscape architecture in Edinburgh and at the time of my last drink, I was washing dishes at a Golf Club for cash in hand. I was thirty-three.

I'd been working and at the end of the night one of the guys said to me "I'm going up to the bar to get a beer. Do you want a beer?" And I said "Yes." The reason that was so shocking was that I hadn't had a drink in twenty-eight days. I'd been to a few AA meetings and I knew I couldn't drink anymore, it was going to kill me. I was very sick from drinking. He asked me the question and I just said "Yes" and I couldn't believe it. I remember drinking that beer really fast and immediately being aware that I wanted another.

They talk in AA about the compulsion to drink. I hadn't thought about it in those terms before but I remember I saw it for what it was at that moment, I was absolutely powerless, and straight away I was up at the bar getting another beer. I had about three or whatever, until they shut the bar. Then I was thinking I need more alcohol but there was no alcohol at home and the bottle shops were closed and I thought I had another friend, "I'll go to their house and see if they'll give me a drink." They'll have alcohol. So I drove over the limit to their house and they knew that I'd been in AA and they knew that I shouldn't drink. I landed at their house at midnight and I asked "Could I have a drink?" they said

"No, you're not supposed to be drinking." Well, I felt so much rage, I couldn't believe it. Like, how dare they? And eventually they said, "OK, you can have one glass of red wine."

Well. That didn't mean anything. I'm alcoholic, you know. I knew what I was going to do. I drank the glass of red wine as quickly as I could. I couldn't have cared too hoots for the friend, to be honest, and this was someone that was a dear friend. At this point, it was just about the alcohol, and when they wouldn't give me anymore I left. I thought, "What am I going to do now?" I needed to keep drinking. I just hadn't had enough. That's the thing when I drink it's never enough. Sometimes alcoholism is referred to as the disease of 'more'.

I needed more alcohol and I thought," I'll call that chef." I'd known this guy for many years. He was a friend of my husband at the time so I called him and said, "Hey, do you mind if I come over for a few drinks or whatever?" I mean, he was shocked I was awake as by this time it must have been 2:00 am. I knew that he'd still be awake and drinking because a lot of hospitality staff go home after work and keep drinking. That wasn't unusual. "You got any drinks?" He said " I got some Coronas in the fridge" and I said, "Great, I'll be there in ten minutes." So again I drove across town and I didn't usually drink and drive.

That was a new low for me in my drinking career because I wasn't a very good driver and had this real fear around driving. So even though I had my drivers license, I only ever drove short distances. But here I was that night drinking and with a compulsion to get more alcohol and driving all over Sydney. I drove to his place.

I couldn't believe it when he said he had beer. He only had a six pack and already he was on the second one, so that only meant like two or three for me. I drank those and then I said "Have you got anything else in the house?" And he said, "No, that's it." I said "Are you sure?" And he replied "My mum's got some wine under the sink, it's white wine she uses for cooking, it's not even cold." And I was like, "Yeah, that'll do." So I had that and there wasn't even that much of that, only a couple glasses. And that was it, I drove home and went to sleep.

The next morning I woke up and I was hungover again. I'd been drinking for twenty years, from thirteen to thirty-three. I was pretty much a daily drinker from the age of nineteen so for me to wake up hungover was not unusual, I was so used to it. I was so used to that sick feeling and not being able to eat anything and I struggled awake, smoked a cigarette, and tried to hold a cup of coffee and piece together the night before. All that is really normal for me, but this time I asked "What will I do? I was really, really confused.

In the twenty-eight days prior to that, I'd been to about six AA meetings and at the second one I'd met this older man called Fred. He would have been in his sixties at the time and he was so kind. I remember he really understood my situation. He let me know this drinking business was very serious which was so bizarre because for a long time I'd known it was serious too.

I felt like people around me, when I tried to raise the issue with them, didn't think so. A lot of people would say, "Oh, you're not that bad." It's that idea of the alcoholic being the man in the park. If you're not drinking in the park or have the bottle in the brown paper bag, you can't possibly be an alcoholic! Even among my own friends and family, they just would say things like "You just need to set a limit for yourself. Try just four drinks. Can you just try and keep it to four, can you?" They were always offering well meaning, kind advice but nothing worked. I knew I couldn't do it. Even my husband at the time would say things like, "Do you have to get so drunk when we go out? Can't you just come home when I go home?" because, I was forever saying "No, no, I'll stay. You go on home." The party could never finish for me.

So I thought, when I told Fred about my drinking he knew it was very important that I not drink. Otherwise it was going to kill me. I remember him saying "For people like us it's death, jail or insanity." And I knew that was the trajectory for me if I didn't stop drinking.

Fred had given me his phone number and I had talked to him a couple of times beforehand. I thought "I'm going to have to call Fred and tell him what happened." I don't know why but I made that phone call and I'm so glad that I did. Fred answered. I think that was the greatest miracle. He's been answering the phone now for fourteen years. He always answers. I told him what had happened the night before and I was so full of shame. I couldn't believe it. I had been so determined to not drink. I thought I'd be doing everything that you were supposed to do, going to meetings and stuff like that.

I had not drank for twenty-eight days. That was huge for me. And yet, I picked up a drink. I thought I was a completely hopeless case. Fred said to me on my phone. "You're not a hopeless case. You're just an alcoholic. And we do it one day at a time. All you have to do is not drink today and go to a meeting tonight."

I was shocked. I actually didn't think they'd let me back in again because I drank. I thought you only got one go at AA and that was it. The one thing that I remember from the first four weeks I was back, I would say things like "My name is Claire, I'm an alcoholic and I'm three days sober ... but I had twenty-eight days," because I felt like they were so hard fought and it was important.

But what I realised was that the second time around there was no more fight. That was a good thing. In AA they talk about surrender, and I threw in the towel because I thought "This is so easy to lose." It really dawned on me that with this sobriety thing, I had to be really vigilant. It's like a flickering flame, and it can be gone so quickly. I actually used to talk about my sobriety as an egg, like a precious egg, and I'm carrying it. The egg not breaking is contingent on me doing certain things that are suggested.

In a way I'm grateful people talk about the 'the bust that you had to have' and some people agree with that, some don't. But for me, I think it was really important because I realise I can't do this on my own. I need other people and need the experience of other people that have gone before me. I need to do what they tell me even when I don't want to do it. There are many, many times that I did not want to go to meetings, especially when my life got really good.

I ended up going back to university and getting my degree. I'm currently doing my Masters. You know, life gets really busy and fantastic when you're sober and it can be hard to find room for meetings or helping other alcoholics or doing the suggested things. One of Fred's words of wisdom is "Don't listen to your head, just do the action."

I started drinking at thirteen, and there was a lot of drinking around me. I grew up in Ireland, there was a lot of drinking and I hated it when big people got drunk. I hated it and I couldn't understand why they would act so idiotic, you know the night before, and then they'd forget it the next morning. I hated that sour smell of hungover parents and, I hated everything, especially not being able to bring friends home. I thought, if I ever drink, when I grow up, I'm never drinking like that. No way. So when I started drinking, I actually thought I was a really good drinker. Because I didn't pass out. You know, I could remember everything the next day. I wasn't vomiting and stumbling all over the place, or talking shit. I wasn't fighting anybody. I was just sort of happy enjoying myself and I could stop before it got atrocious. And that continued for a few years.

They talk about alcoholism being progressive and my drinking progressed. The more it changed, the more confused I became because I couldn't understand. "Why all of a sudden was I the most drunk person in the room? Why was I getting drunk?" That was not my intention. I never set out to get drunk, ever. I never said I'm going to get smashed tonight or I'm going to tie one on. No way. I loved drinking. I love the feeling it gave me because I was a really intense, anxious child and I still can be a very intense person and I loved that when I had a drink my shoulders fell down from my ears and they relaxed. I loved that feeling.

I think what makes me an alcoholic is I'm powerless over alcohol. When I drink, I can't guarantee my behaviour and that characterised the last ten years of my drinking. I think what is really sad is that in my early twenties I knew I had a problem. I ended up making a conscious decision to have a child because I thought that was going to fix me. That's what I needed to do. That was going to slow me down. I needed someone to love and someone that would love me.

When I turned twenty-three, my eldest daughter was born. And it was very difficult being a mother, all my family were back in Ireland

and it was a very, very lonely time and alcohol helped. Drinking on my own had already started. When I first arrived in Australia at nineteen, I drank to cure homesickness. I found that worked. At thirty-three when I was washing dishes in the Golf Club, I had two daughters and they were five and ten. I genuinely thought that they would be better off without me and that is what is so soul destroying about being an alcoholic mum. You can't look yourself in the eyes. You can't look your children in their eyes. I would wake up hungover, as a mum.

I remember one time I had fallen over at a hospitality work function. I had fallen over because I'd been drinking. I didn't know I was drunk but when I arrived at the hospital the nurse wrote 'intoxicated' on my paperwork and I was so ashamed and outraged. I got thirteen stitches in my head that night and I remember coming home and I lay on the lounge. The next morning, my youngest daughter would have been about two and oldest daughter would have been about six, and they both came over with their little kids hands, little soft spongy, little hands, so clean and white and they're rubbing my forehead going "OK, mummy, OK" and I just wanted to die. I really wanted to die. It was a terrible feeling. It's hard to keep fronting up as a mother when you're hungover and you've done things the night before that you can't remember. It's very hard to try and act normally and get the kids ready and get them at the school or to preschool.

That's why when I met Fred he knew that things hadn't been OK for me. He knew that they hadn't been OK for a very long time, and that to me, was such a relief.

> **Clare** is the mother of two daughters, who she loves dearly, both of whom are at university. Clare is currently completing her Masters in Social Work.

10

Michael B

As an active alcoholic I had many dramatic nights where I thought "Enough was enough." In the end my last drink wasn't particularly specular but it was life changing.

I was sitting on the veranda of my beautiful Queenslander in Brisbane, drinking beer by myself as had become my normal daily routine. On this occasion I was overcome with sadness and desperation, the alcohol was offering me no relief for the emptiness and loneliness I was running away from. I had real tears swelling in my eyes because all I felt was the desperate need not to feel anything. I had almost drunk an entire carton of beer that day and only had a couple of beers left and had accepted that despite myself, I would have to get back into the car to purchase more alcohol to make it through the night. In a blackout I drove to and from the bottle shop and continued to drink until I passed out.

To this day I cannot explain why that was the turning point. I had driven in blackout many times before and I had cried in desperation many times before that too. On this occasion, I sensed that "It was over," that the alcohol no longer offered respite from my pain and that from this point on, it would only add to the misery I was feeling. I was fortunate enough to have recognised that my life, which was already unmanageable, was spiralling out of control and it was going to get worse if I continued to drink.

I had recognised that I had a problem a few years earlier and had tried to moderate my drinking behaviour. I tried to drink light beer, buy lesser amounts, only on weekends etc ... but I found that once I had the first drink, I was compelled to keep drinking. I was unwilling or unable to stop until I ran out of alcohol or passed out from it. I had tried self-help books and audio tapes, watched YouTube videos, joined online groups and had hypnotherapy but nothing worked longer than a few days. I had even been aware of AA for a number of years and had tried half heartedly to work with them in the past.

Like many teenagers growing up in Ireland, I drank excessively at all social occasions, but it didn't interfere with anything I needed to do. I played sports, dated girls, finished school, started working and had a very normal life. In Ireland I was vaguely aware of AA. Being a dropdown drunk was considered to be unfortunate, but to be a member of AA was considered failure and to be pitied. I left Ireland to go to college in New York and my drinking slowed down because I was on an athletic program, studying and working. After college I worked in London and drank socially because I didn't want to be the caricature Irish drunk.

When I migrated to Australia my drinking behaviour changed. Something about Australia suggested that the rules were different. Every event offered the opportunity to drink alcohol. Birthdays, bar-b-ques, christenings, work functions, luncheons; all featured alcohol and I was only too happy to embrace that aspect of the culture.

I was successful in business and relationships for a while, but in my late forties things started to unravel. My marriage was unfulfilling, my business was struggling, and I had made a few bad investments. I hadn't realised how much I was drinking, but on reflection, it had been a slow, steady increase over the years towards the end. At this point, alcohol still provided a pleasant distraction from all the various issues that I was unwilling to address in my life. I pretended that life was manageable and that I would get myself together and if I had a drink I'd settle down and it would all be OK in the morning. But the issues were mounting, nothing was getting resolved, I needed increasingly larger amounts of alcohol to find relief until I had that final drink.

When I returned to AA, I understood I had a problem that I couldn't address by myself. I recognised that once I started drinking, I didn't have the ability to stop. It wasn't so much that I couldn't stop, it was that once I started, I no longer contemplated stopping until blackout. This acceptance made my experience in AA much easier. I was also fortunate to meet a number of older sober members who I connected with and whom I felt wanted me to get better. I was at the point of surrender where AA seems to be at its most effective. For the first time in many years, I experienced a sense of hope that I would get better if I stuck close to these people.

I have been sober for four years. I found the first few months to be exceedingly difficult. Despite all the encouragement I was receiving and being aware of the need to change, I longed for the relief that I once found from alcohol, many years before. I was fortunate though to find an incredibly supportive band of members who allowed me to fumble and find my own way in AA.

Being a member of AA didn't address any of the issues that I was struggling with. My marriage was still unsatisfactory, my business was broken, and I had lots of debts. Being sober, however, has enabled me to look at each of these issues, acknowledge where I was responsible and to take action to fix them.

Total abstinence from alcohol, being an active member of AA community, addressing all my outstanding issues in a responsible manner, and making plans for the future have given me another opportunity at life for which I'm very grateful.

> **Michael** is a father and business owner, who has lived, studied, travelled, and worked on three continents. His interests include sports, community activism and he plays music in a covers band.

11

Fred T

My name is Fred and I'm an alcoholic. I'm a member of Talopea, Wednesday night AA. The date of my sobriety is the 26th September 1979. What got me to AA was the horrors of drinking. I only drank for ten years and three months and the last week of my drinking was very much like the last year of my drinking. It was horrific.

When I picked up one drink which I did every day, my life went completely out of whack. There was no way I could have one drink and stop. I was at the stage that every time I drank I went into a blackout and I did things that I'm still ashamed of. I had a wife and four young children at the time. I was in business and I insulted my customers, insulted everyone I dealt with and that was all I could think about in that last week of my drinking. I was still working up until the Sunday before I stopped drinking because I drank every day at work and I worked for myself. I finished the day in a blackout. Sunday 23rd September was my thirty-ninth birthday and I drank as much as normal which is as much as I could possibly drink.

Something changed in my life though because I always said "I'm not an alcoholic because I could always get to work," and from that day on I could not get out of the house. I was filled with fear and anxiety. I'd drink myself into a blackout and come out of a blackout and drink more and my wife and children were terrified and didn't know what to say or what to do. When the phone rang and my wife said someone wants you I couldn't answer the phone or do anything.

I don't remember anything about that 26th September or the days before, except what my wife and other people told me. I remember coming out of a blackout briefly and I was lying on the lounge in the living room and my wife and sister were across from me and my sister said "What's going to happen here," and my wife said "I think he's going to die and that will be good," and my sister said "Yes, he probably will, that's right." Then I went back into a blackout and when I came too again my sister had gone and my wife had put the kids to bed because I was sleeping on the lounge. I'd been out of the bedroom for a few years. I was sleeping with a loaded shotgun under the lounge because I knew someone was coming to get me.

I came out of that blackout about 9:00 pm and I sat there and thought, "So I can't live with a drink and I can't live without a drink." Then I thought, "Well I've got the shotgun," and I put it in my mouth and was about to pull the trigger and then I don't know what got into me. It had nothing to do with religion or anything else, I just said "God help me" and then I said to myself "Alcohol is my problem," and then a series of things happened.

I went to my family doctor the next morning and I was as sick as a mongrel dog and I told him the truth and he listened to me for forty minutes and he was a real gentleman. I never heard him swear before and he just said "Fred, you're a fucking alcoholic, there's nothing else I can do for you. Simply go to AA or don't come back to me." And that was where I went.

The things that happened to me is why I'm still here today and the background to that is, I had never had a drink until I was twenty-eight years and nine months of age because I was always told if I drank I would be an alcoholic. My father never had a drink in his life and he was a great friend with Father Tom, who was one of the founders of AA. As everyone knows Tom drank until 1952. My father said to me a few times that Tom said to him "If Fred drinks he will be worse than me" and he said "I knew how bad Tom was and if you drink you will be as bad as Tom." So I never drank. I was raised in the bush and left school at twelve years of age and when we worked together my father said to me "You must be drinking mate because you're such a moody bastard." That was me waiting for a drink, just like Tom said.

Tom was always a good friend of the family and got to meet Doctor Minogue (early AA supporter). My mum also had a very strong attachment and admired Dr Minogue. I said to my father once "She doesn't mention Minogue anymore" and he told me later on that Minogue said to my mother "We will see Freddie in AA one day," she never mentioned him again. It was great to be a friend of this great doctor but he got crossed off the list.

Minogue wasn't wrong by the way because from the first drink I had a total personality change. I was a teetotaller, a wowser and never went into pubs or clubs. I worked in a winery and never had a drink there. I always had good quality wine at my house because we lived on Penfold's property and I had to entertain people that came. The morning my first daughter was born, I can still remember that moment clearly, I opened a bottle of red. I'd been working in that winery for five years at the time and I never ever thought of having a drink. I walked down to the cellars at six o'clock that morning to open up for the early starters and one old bloke said "Fred you look different today" and I know now when I had a drink I changed completely.

All that day I remember I was thinking "When I get home tonight I can finish that bottle." Alcohol switched my brain to a completely different area. I got home that night, I finished that bottle and the next one and the next one and the next one. I was finishing bottles for ten years and three months and I was always a blackout drinker. I was hospitalised a few times for panic attacks when I didn't have my morning drinks. I always had to have that morning drink.

With that first drink two things happened immediately, the compulsion to drink and a total personality change. Before that I was a good Catholic man, married, had my first child and had a responsible job at Penfold's. From that first drink, I forgot I was married, I forgot to pay our taxes, I forgot that you don't steal from the boss. I forgot all of those things.

And yeah, after a few years, I'd left the wine industry because I had a good name and I didn't want to get the sack. I worked for myself on my cell phone and went door to door around the western suburbs. But the amounts that I drank, the things that I did, you know they say you can forget the past but I can't forget the past and it's been forty-two and a half years since I had my last drink. There are still things that I regret very much.

Alcoholism is such an horrific disease. This morning, I spoke to a girl who's coming back to AA after having a four month bust, and my God, this woman is highly intelligent and motivated. She has a good business, and is a multi-millionaire. She had one drink the other day and she totally transformed from a smart woman to a raging bloody idiot. That was me, one drink and you're gone mate.

I've gone regularly to AA and nowadays I do six meetings a week. While I was working I did a meeting every second night, so it was three one week and four the other. My wife passed away eighteen months ago and the last thing she said to me was "Don't give up the meetings" and I'll never give up the meetings. You know my marriage only lasted because I got sober. I was told that the AA program was a hard, tough program, but it works if I'm willing to do what I'm told.

My doctor had said to me, yeah, go to AA but don't come back to me, I can't stand whingeing bloody drunks and I said "How do I find it?" He said "If you want it bad enough you'll find it yourself. Nobody can do it for you." So I went home, looked in the Yellow Pages and rang AA Central office. They gave me two meetings. One was up the road from me at Baulkham Hills and I thought "I'm not going there. I don't want people to know I'm alcoholic." Everyone in the district knew I was a raging alcoholic. I'd arrive at the National Bank on Monday morning with all this cash, if I hadn't been gambling or drinking and the teller would say "Mr Fred, please stand back, I can't stand the fumes." But I wouldn't go to the Baulkham Hills meeting. The second meeting was North Ryde on Thursday night next to the Catholic Church. So I went to that one and I don't know why I was just so sick. I knew I was shivering and shaking. The doctor put me on Valium, and I swallowed a couple of Valium, parked my old Holden around the corner from the church so nobody recognised me and staggered into the hall.

This bloke, I thought he was a bank manager, and I still see him today, was the secretary and he had a nice shirt on and a green sleeveless jumper. And he just said "Welcome, we've been waiting for you." I thought anyone waiting for me was waiting around the corner with a pick handle or something like that. They were very simple things. I didn't know what to do or what to say, and he said, "Do you have a problem with alcohol? If so, you're in the right place, mate. Welcome, go sit near that bloke with the tattoos" and then he said "Take the cotton wool out of your ears and put it in your mouth and you might hear something that might save your life."

That's the story, I sat in that meeting, shivering and shaking. I was going to get up and walk out and he just put his hand on my shoulder and said "Never walk out of a meeting, son." He was calling me son and he's ten years younger than me. Anyway, at the end of the meeting he gave me the AA Big Book and I said "What do I do with this?" and he said "You read the fucking thing mate" and I said "What if I don't?" He said "If you don't you will die and we will go to your funeral." Then a lady came up to me, a very nice but tough lady and she said "I'll be your sponsor until you find somebody else," and she was my sponsor for thirty-six years until she passed away. I was just blessed or lucky to get the right people at the right time, because from that moment she spent a lot of time with me, my wife, and our children. She was also a member of Al-anon. Her husband died and never got sober. From that first meeting, I knew there was nowhere else to go. I can't say I wanted to be in AA, I can't say that I walked in that door and felt at home like some people say, I just sat there and thought, "Well, these blokes are not drinking and there's hope for me."

There were not that many people who had really long term sobriety back then, my sponsor had fifteen years. In AA they say do what is suggested, and I was sick enough to do what I was told. My sponsor told me what to do and if I questioned her she would say "When you come back from the pub, give me a call." She told me to "Go to meetings, and when you're stressed, say the serenity prayer." I still say it about a hundred times a day, and it seems to be working now. It's the only prayer that works for me, it's unbelievable.

I just love newcomers. I support a lot of people. I'm currently sponsoring about eight people who have sobriety from one day to about thirteen years. Chapter 7 in the Big Book states "My sobriety is dependent on carrying the message to another alcoholic," and I think that works. I think that's why they looked after me. I thought they looked after me because I was a great bloke myself but they were trying to stay sober themselves. So, we stay sober by helping somebody else, I think that's the way it runs, mate.

> **Fred** retired at 78 after being self-employed for fifty years. He has four children, six grandchildren, and has been a member of the Talopea AA meeting for 32 years.

12

Ian Westaway

I got introduced to AA when I was twenty-one or twenty-two, so I didn't get sober from my first meeting but I was sort of going to AA meetings. For the first time in my life I met other people who didn't drink. Apart from my dad I never knew anyone who didn't drink, but I wasn't ready to stop drinking, I wasn't ready to hand in the towel or to surrender.

I didn't think they were like me. I thought I was the worst person in the world. I thought they were like saints. Keep in mind, in those days everybody was a lot older. I was in my early twenties. It's a different thing nowadays, but the bottom line is I wasn't ready. I hadn't been kicked around enough to stop or to want to stop.

The last couple of years I went down, down, down, but I didn't see myself going down and I couldn't do anything about it, alcohol dictated the terms of my life. I thought I was the smartest bloke in the world, but by the time I got to AA I had grave doubts about how clever I was.

The last couple of years were the barren, hard years and I was really drinking for oblivion. I had a physical compulsion coupled with a mental obsession for alcohol and I couldn't stop from starting. That was my problem.

I had all the troubles of the world, I had no money. I was full of fear and remorse but once I got a couple of drinks into me the light went on and I was all right. I say all right, but I was on the merry-go-round again.

I would get into all these situations. I would get pissed and run a car into another car. To me they were irritations of my drinking. But the trouble was, I was on a bender for about six weeks but I was 'gone from the grog', I was flat out getting a kick out of it.

I was on a bender in Manly for about six weeks. The last twenty-four hours I was barred from the clubs and pubs in the district. I got into the Diggers Club and I had an argument with the manager, all in a blackout because I don't remember a lot of it. I ended up at Manly wharf. In those days they had the big wooden ferries. They had high pressure hoses on the walls and when the ferry pulled up I was spraying the people getting off the ferry with the hose. Unbeknown to me my future wife Jan was on the ferry and was completely embarrassed.

I was about eleven stone and could hardly walk but I had enough strength to do that. So the cops came from everywhere and obviously locked me up and that was the last drink I had. What happened is that they sent me to Long Bay gaol for six weeks and that was the best thing that could have happened. Because when I got there I felt safe and I was glad to be there. I started to feel well and I remember thinking I have to go back to AA. I also thought I was going to die but I wasn't afraid of dying; I was sick of the rehearsals. I was sick of the vomiting and the poverty and shivers and shakes and everything else, and I was twenty-seven years old.

So in actual fact I didn't stop, I was stopped, but for the first time in my life I had made a decision and I didn't realise it until I'd been in AA for two years.

My father was one of the earliest founding members of the Narrabeen meeting. He got sober when I was ten years old. I am a typical alcoholic. We have this terrible blind spot to alcohol, don't we? I mean, if it wasn't for him introducing me to AA, I would have been dead, you know. I can never repay him for looking after me. To put up with a practising alcoholic is a terrible thing. I can see it looking back. He was a builder like me, but then I was a carpenter so I did an apprenticeship under him.

He was always there for me, you know what I mean? Like he protected me and the other kids. You see, there was a long history of alcoholism in the family. I really believe I was born with alcoholism because of my grandmother's brothers, I never met either of them. One of them was killed on a motorbike and another one burnt himself to death with a lit cigarette when he was drunk and fell asleep.

Then I started going to the meetings. Coming into AA, I was left with myself, I couldn't sit on the chairs, I couldn't stand up, I couldn't do anything. I was like a train wreck that hit a rock wall, it was the wreckage of my life.

At first, I had no peace of mind. People talked about peace of mind but I didn't understand what they were talking about. The thing is, in hindsight, I surrendered and I was willing. They said 'how it worked' was to practise honesty, open mindedness and willingness, and I was willing to go to any length as I didn't have anywhere else to go. I was at the end of my road.

I walked into a meeting slightly late one night and a guy who was in the chair said "If you're here tonight and if you're sick and tired of being sick and tired, you're in the right place" and those words have never left me.

And then a couple of months later I heard "You can leave this meeting tonight and need not drink again and be happy about it." That was like winning the lottery, it had been said thousands of times before but I could never hear it. It's like anything, you can't hear it until you can hear it. I got hope from the guy saying that, then I started to get faith but I couldn't put names on those things.

They said, "You have to do two things. You have to not drink and go to meetings." And those two things still stand today! There's no substitute for meetings! Now I'm 76.

Ian is a well known Sydney builder. He regularly attends the Sunday night AA meeting at Narrabeen which was co-founded by his father Jack decades ago.

13

Ruth F

That last drink I ever had was nothing much. No shame, no danger, no injuries, just a drunken night out like many other drunken nights. It was a Tuesday night, and I went out to dinner with some work friends. One of those friends was a bit of a drinker, so of course we got on tremendously and we had a fine old evening. On the way home in a taxi, I told the driver to take a route that made no sense. In a city that I'd lived in for many years I was lost. That's hardly the worst thing that ever happened to me, but for all its banality it crushed me, and was the drink that led me to my first AA meeting.

If I think back further to before that last night and my first AA meeting, I can now see how increasingly disordered my life had become. For many years I would have said I lived a normal life. If I'd even thought to mention my drinking (which I wouldn't) I'd have said it was nothing out of the ordinary. The pathway to emotional ruin through drinking was slow, restrained for many years by the love of a close family, the society of kind friends, a good education, travel and a genuine interest in the world. Throughout those years drinking seemed to cost me nothing but money. For me alcoholism was a disease that spread slowly, culminating in a quick and devastating fall. In a matter of months my world unraveled. A gnawing restlessness took hold of me, and drinking became a way of managing dread. At night, drunk, I would slip into blackness and wake with no recollection of dreams, not even the faintest outline of them.

Those last few months were painful and bewildering, yet something else was happening at the same time. I had fallen into the orbit of a sober member of AA, and he became my friend. He told me what had happened to him, how it felt to be an alcoholic and what his life was like as a sober man. One day he asked me how much I knew about myself, and I responded that I knew myself inside out. The correct answer to that question was in fact the opposite – I knew embarrassingly little about myself, including the fact that I was an alcoholic. He knew what I did not, but he didn't lecture or judge me and in speaking to him I found consolation. Something like hope came to me through his stories, and also in what I thought was a chance attendance at a public lecture.

My AA friend invited me to the event, and I accepted because the historian and the topic were of interest. What I didn't know was that the speaker was also a sober member of AA and that I was being set up. At some point during the lecture the historian abandoned the topic and started talking instead about his drinking and how he got sober. "Strange," I thought, yet not jarring because he somehow managed to weave his drinking story into a lecture about the political history of Brisbane. What really was peculiar though, was the sense that he was talking to me. I was seated at the front (no accident I now know) and it felt as though he was looking straight at me! It should have made me feel uncomfortable but instead I was riveted. I left the lecture almost euphoric with no idea why. He was an accomplished speaker, no doubt, but that wasn't it; I was sure that something else had happened. What I know now, is that I had identified with the story of a sober alcoholic and that a sense of belonging was taking root in my heart.

I had been a hopeful sort of character all my life but in truth that hope was often just magical thinking. Somehow things were going to turn out in my favour but not because of any effort on my part. This blissful state would just materialise. Going to that lecture and hearing that alcoholic tell his story was magic of a sort, but it wasn't enough to make me stop drinking then. It planted the seed, however, so when I came to my last dreary drink, and I was too scared and exhausted to keep going as I was, I knew there was another way. The morning after my last night, I woke up hungover and I didn't drink that day. That wasn't so remarkable, I could still go a day or two without drinking; what was remarkable was that I had the beginning of a notion that I couldn't drink ever again. I rang my AA friend and said, "You know those meetings you go to, I think I need to go to one." So he took me to the Wednesday 8:00 pm St Lucia meeting of Alcoholics Anonymous.

Unlike most AA members I don't know the exact date I got sober. There are a couple reasons for that, firstly the concept of a 'sobriety date' annoyed me, so I refused to have one. Secondly, I continued to use drugs other than alcohol because the prospect of living unanaesthetised was more than I could bear. In time, and with the help of older, sober members of AA, I came to see that only through complete abstinence from all mind-altering drugs could I begin the journey to the decent, purposeful life I'd imagined for myself but didn't really know how to achieve. Still, my oppositional defiance led me not to acknowledge that date either. The best I can say is that sometime around the middle of January 1996, I gave it all away.

That St Lucia meeting closed many years ago but if I try, I can see the room, half-lit, with eight or nine sober strangers seated around the walls. I can recall how frightened I was to be in that room, but how relieved I was too. I'd gone along to the meeting still holding out hope that I wouldn't fit in, that identifying with a couple sober alcoholics was an irregularity. I was simultaneously horrified and intensely grateful to find that I did belong, that I was with my kind. For twenty-six years I've stuck close to AA and have found it much more to my liking than I first thought. I remain an imperfect person, but I am no longer baffled by life. Serenity is a big word, but some days I have it. I am, and always will be an alcoholic – in that I have no choice. My choice is to be drunk or sober and today I choose sober.

> **Ruth** is a Queenslander who grew up in the outback. She lived in Brisbane for many years before moving to the North of England, but returns often to Australian shores.

14

Deb S

I picked up my first drink when I was sixteen. My mother, in an act she will never forgive herself for, had a party and allowed me to have a drink. I didn't have one drink, I got blind drunk and was transported to another world. I was a shy, lost, lonely, frightened girl and that changed with that first drink. I had my first blackout, and the anxiety left. I went from being a wallflower to being the life of a party. I honestly, deeply, in my soul, believed that with alcohol inside me, anything was possible.

Within a week I was drinking every day and soon drinking every morning before school. I went from the A student in every subject to being the person most likely to die. It was such a dramatic fall from grace for me.

Shortly after my first drink, I had a run in with the police. I learned I could keep out of serious trouble by keeping away from people. I took to drinking secretly in public toilets and railway stations. By seventeen I was in full flight.

My parents put a lock on the bedroom door and nailed my window shut, to protect me from the inevitable, me running away and getting into dangerous situations. Around that time I was sexually abused by a teacher. He would pick me up on Saturday mornings and take me to a park. He would give me two bottles of alcohol and then take me to a hotel to do whatever he damn liked. That abuse sped up the descent into alcoholism because I couldn't handle the guilt.

My mother took me to a psychiatrist, psychologist, hypnotherapist, you name it, looking for the answer. I was so deeply ashamed, I never told those people the truth. I'd be put into psychiatric institutions, giving my parents hope, "Maybe this time it'll be different." I knew it wouldn't be different because I had to have alcohol. I had over twenty psychiatric admissions in five years, and eight suicide attempts. Whenever I could I'd run away. My parents or the police would find me and take me home. My parents looked after me and by the end of my drinking, I couldn't leave the house. I'd call a taxi to bring booze.

By twenty I'd been drinking for almost five years without trying to stop. I couldn't imagine life without alcohol, all that mattered to me was me. I had no awareness of the damage I was doing to anyone around me and didn't care.

I couldn't leave the house and had to hide the bottles, what a challenge. We had an above ground swimming pool with decking around it. Some of the palings had come loose, so I tossed my empties under there - for a long time. One night there was a massive storm and the next day the pool had collapsed and the backyard was a mass of floating bottles. I took one look thought "Fuck! I can't get rid of these empties."

So I waited, I knew I would get the lecture. "What's the matter with you? Pull your socks up. You've got so much willpower, why can't you stop drinking?" I was immune to it, like water off a duck's back. I waited but it didn't come. My father sat down, elbows on his knees and chin in his hands and tears rolling down his face. This completely did me in. He was an unemotional man. I had never seen him cry before, or since.

For the first time I saw what I was doing to the people that loved me. My parents no longer had guests or entertained anyone because of me. My nine year old brother was wetting the bed every night because of me. The fighting and turbulence in my home centred around me and I couldn't deal with it.

I was overwhelmed and waited until everyone had gone to work and ordered two bottles of vodka. I'd stashed a box of antidepressants and took the pills and vodka and laid down to die. I didn't write a note. I had to suicide because I knew I would continue living this way and couldn't stop drinking. I woke up in hospital. My mother had come home from work and found me. I remember thinking "I can't even kill myself, I'm useless."

When I came home I didn't participate in the family. I sat in a little arm chair in the dining room and the family lived around me, I wasn't included. I knew I couldn't continue like this. I no longer had any pills, and was too much of a coward to throw myself off a bridge or lay down on railway tracks. I needed an easier, softer way out of it.

I rang my GP and was honest about my drinking for the first time. It happened that he knew a doctor who was a member of Alcoholics Anonymous. He said I had to go into rehab, and that petrified me. I'd had so many psychiatric admissions, but had never been in rehab. I was booked into hospital the next day and being a typical alcoholic I thought, "I need a final drink." I got a flagon of medium dry sherry because it was $0.99, so cheap. The taxi brought it and I drank half the flagon. Then I went into the linen cupboard and made a hole in the wall and hid the bottle, in case I needed it later. Flagons are really hard to hide.

I went into a blackout and woke up the following morning, lying in a hospital bed fully clothed. I didn't know where I was, I thought "I'm back in another psych ward" then fell asleep again. When I woke up I realised I was in rehab.

I was introduced to AA and the miracle worked at my very first meeting, I identified. I accepted the fact that I was an alcoholic. I accepted the first step in its entirety, that I was powerless. I was in rehab for eight weeks and went to meetings every night. After the meetings I'd sit on the end of my bed and think "Knowing my luck, I'll live to a hundred, that's eighty years without a drink." I thought being in AA with these old people was the end of my life. But I made a deal with myself, "If that flagon is in that hiding spot when I get home, then it's on again. I'll drink it. But if that bottle is gone I will keep this on." My mother found that bottle and threw it out. I kept that promise. I was twenty when I had my last drink.

I met my sponsor at my first meeting. I had two black eyes because I was a fall down drunk. She sat down next to me and reached out and held my hand. I remember thinking "When was the last time anyone touched me?" It was an overwhelming feeling. She told me she saw herself in me and encouraged me to join a group immediately. I joined the Ramsgate AA meeting. I had no way of getting to meetings so members organised a roster and someone would pick me up daily. On the way to the meeting they would tell me their stories and talk about sobriety. I really wanted to tell them to piss off but I was such a people pleaser I didn't have the courage to and went along with it. And thank God I did. They were infinitely kind, patient, and gracious.

I was told not to get involved with anyone in my first year and I thought, "What would you old farts know?" I cast my eyes around the meeting, and picked out two blokes. I said to myself "The first one to ask me out, you're the one for me." Then one guy asked me out. He was twenty-two years older than me, an active member of the Communist Party, waterfront worker, convicted armed robber, an active drug user, and a violent man. He was a very sick man but I didn't know that at the time. I was determined that I was going to make that relationship work. Everyone told me I was doing the wrong thing. He was violent, threw me through a window once and used to beat the crap out of me. He reinforced the way I felt about myself, how useless I was.

When that relationship started to fall apart I thought "I know the answer to this, I'll have a baby." I purposely fell pregnant because in my warped mind I thought if we had a baby it would tether him to me forever. When my daughter was seven months old she died. I was two and a half years sober and thought that everything I'd worked for in sobriety had been taken away from me.

I learned from that experience that my best thinking gets me into trouble, I made bad decisions and wrong choices. I was going to either pick up a drink or get stuck into the program. I bought a bottle of vodka, had the lid off the bottle and planned to go to the park and drink it, but for some reason I picked up the phone and rang my sponsor. That's when my journey started.

I am who I am. I'm stubborn, rebellious, and wilful, but desperately wanted to feel differently to how I felt. I was still lonely and full of fear. I was still having panic attacks. I wanted to be like everyone else. I couldn't get sober until I became willing to do whatever it took.

It took a disaster, which was a kind of an awakening, a real turning point for me. I struggled with the concept of a Higher Power for a long time. I didn't have a religious upbringing, and God was never mentioned at home. So I had no concept. Members suggested "Why don't you get on your knees and pray?" I did but felt stupid, like a fraud. "How do I know what's God's will and what's mine? How do I know the messages I think I'm getting?" I had to learn to check my thinking with other people. I asked "What's the difference between what I want and what I need?" I started to make good choices in my life.

A string of circumstances led to me relapsing. I was twenty-three years sober when my sponsor died, and I never replaced her, and was bottling everything up inside me. I was the person that everyone came to but I didn't have anyone to go to. I had pneumonia three times in one year and developed a heart problem. I had to start medication that made me feel foggy and I wasn't allowed to exercise. I didn't realise the effect that had on me. I used to communicate with my Higher Power and ask for guidance when I walked in the morning. I stopped doing that and I wasn't checking my thinking with anyone. I think the biggest problem with relapsing was losing my identity. I'd been a sober alcoholic in AA and once I drank, I wasn't. "Who in the hell was I?" I called everything into question, and it took a long time to come to terms with. I'll never be happy about relapsing and have to accept that it's part of the illness and now part of my story.

As they say in AA alcohol is cunning, baffling, and powerful.

> **Deb** is a senior executive in the financial services industry. She enjoys travel, volunteering in the community, exercise, and a good game of rugby league with her beloved Sharks. A keen seamstress, Deb makes her own clothes and is a doting grandmother to two kids.

15

Norma Christian

My name is Norma and I started drinking at age seventeen. I was a quiet young person and terrified of authority, but when I picked up a drink that certainly changed my life, as did joining AA. I came from a poor working class family in Scotland and we lived in the tenements and poverty was prevalent in my life. I had no career prospects and saw an advert in the paper to join the Army and to do nursing training. So I joined the British Army and was based in Germany for three years. Joining the army was fantastic, I was able to have a shower everyday, have my own room, and I learnt to drink alcohol. I loved the drinking, I felt it gave me a fantastic personality. It wired me up and I could talk to anybody.

After three years of being in Germany I was posted to Hong Kong. I put on weight in Germany with all that beer and everything else I consumed, and someone suggested I take some pills to help lose weight. They were amphetamines and I became instantly addicted. So for two years I took those pills and it was fantastic. I became a skinny minny.

After five years in the Army, I met a bloke, a drinker up in Scotland and we decided through circumstances to get married and come to Australia. He was constantly out of work and with my nursing qualifications I became the main breadwinner. After the third child was born he lost another job. It was in the news that he had broken a woman's arm when he was at work so I told him to leave, and I got a housing commission flat and went on the pension.

I had three little children and lived in housing commission and because I was drinking and smoking and wanted to go out socialising the pension hardly covered expenses. I was in my early thirties and the money was running out very quickly and somebody told me to go to the charities. I went to the Smith family, Salvation Army, every charity I could think of to get money. I professed to be a great mother, but I was an absolute shocker. So anyway, these dear old ladies said to me that if I went to their meeting they would give my daughter a bursary. I went to that meeting and I think I took some beers with me and smelled of drink. The ladies were truly shocked because I took my three children to the meeting.

They sent a minister to my home that afternoon and he said to me "I believe you've got a drinking problem," but I didn't think I had a drinking problem. I thought the drink was the only thing that saved me and got me through difficult days with these children. He said to me "You need to go to AA now." I was an atheist and I was truly shocked. This minister said to me, "You have to get on the phone now, I'm waiting here until you contact Alcoholics Anonymous." I thought that was absolutely shocking, fancy me being an alcoholic, that couldn't apply to me surely.

Alcoholics Anonymous was the first entry in the phone book in those days, so I rang them and said "I think I've got a drinking problem." They got in touch with a person who was willing to 'Twelfth Step' me and she rang up and said, "Oh, I'll take you to a meeting tonight." I replied "No, no, no, I can't go because I have these little children." She said, "Don't worry, I'll bring a babysitter." She brought her teenage son along to babysit and I went to my first AA meeting at South Hurstville. She sat me in the front row and I just cried and cried.

I knew they were saying abstinence but I thought "AA might be like Weight Watchers, you go for six weeks and moderate your drinking." I had begun to drink from morning till night, sip, sip, sip, all through the day, in a brown coffee cup, because if somebody came in they could see I was drinking coffee. But the alcohol was leaking out of my pores along with the cigarettes.

This lady, Maureen, continued to take me to meetings for three months and then I said "I will be alright now." Of course I had decided to try and drink moderately by myself. Once I got the alcohol back into me, it was on again, and that is the shameful part of my story. I had these little children. The boys were two and four and my daughter was nine and I was back out drinking, drinking, drinking. I had a little part time job that was helping me because I didn't want to go around the charities again.

What happened after eighteen months is this, it was shameful. I brought all sorts of different types into the house, exposed my children to danger and after eighteen months, I had a big car smash. I lost my drivers license, lost that little job, and I knew I had to go back to AA. That was thirty-eight years ago. In 1983 I came back to the fellowship.

Then miracles started to happen. Being an atheist had stopped me for many years, I couldn't go to those groups that had the 'God' word in them, I forgot about that and came back to the fellowship. Around then, somebody said to me there's a little psychiatric hospital in Kogarah, looking for a night nurse and I went there to get that job. That was my last sip of wine. I had to have a drink to sign the application papers, because I had tremors coming off the alcohol.

That was my very, very last drink because I got that job, and that psychiatric place happened to be a detox and it was marvellous. I worked with a doctor who was in the fellowship, and the Matron was in the fellowship, and I was just surrounded by people who cared about AA. You know nowadays it's all this harm minimisation stuff in the health department, they don't talk much about AA, but it helped me then and it's helping me now in 2022.

I was there for ten years, part time. I also did a couple of university degrees at that time as well. I wanted to get a good job to give my children a better future than I had had. Eventually I became a clinical nurse specialist in mental health at a teaching hospital, St George Hospital Sydney, and I was there for twenty years.

I'm still very involved in the fellowship and continue to help. I run a couple of meetings and it's great to see people like Ross with 53 years of sobriety. Thank you to AA for helping me and my family.

Norma Christian is a retired mental health nurse and secretary to an AA meeting in Sydney.

16

Kym

When I was thinking back about my last drink, I mean it's sixteen years ago and a little bit blurry now, but I still remember some things, the day to day, every day at the end of my drinking was the same. I would wake up still pretty drunk and I always had alcoholic diarrhoea. I was a wreck. I'd wake up with this really crippling depression. My first thought of the morning would be like self hatred thoughts. Thinking I was pathetic and "Why couldn't I fix this problem?" That was the immediate thought I'd have when I'd wake up and that was followed by me making promises to myself, "This is going to be the day that I'm going to get on top of this problem."

This was a daily pattern of thoughts and feelings that I'd have, every morning, and making these promises to myself. I don't remember making promises to other people, but I remember always making them to myself. I always started out with that intention, in the grip of depression, that I was going to do something and this was going to be the day.

I would be sick for hours in the morning and later get some food down and eat something greasy, just to line my stomach. Then I'd be going about my day and probably start sobering up in the afternoon, keeping in mind that I had little kids to look after. So my kids were like three and six. I would be running around going to school, dropping them off at daycare, going to work, busy doing all this stuff, but in the afternoon the anxiety would build up and it only occurred to me recently, that was my trigger.

The anxiety was a killer, you know, depression was easier for me to deal with. My anxiety would build and build and I was so overwhelmed. I was bringing up kids, doing all this stuff, getting dinners ready, getting school clothes sorted, and I just couldn't bear it. It was just always so overwhelming and then around that time of day, my thinking would start changing and there wouldn't be a resolution in sight. It would all be a good reason to get into this deep resentment mode.

I remember thinking "Anybody in this situation that has to deal with what I have to deal with would drink. I deserve to drink because of what I have to put up with because this is so fucking hard, what I'm doing." Or just, "Fuck It!" like, you know, "Who fucking cares." You know, if I didn't have alcohol in the house I would go and get it and then I'd start drinking. And when I started drinking I just couldn't get enough into me, and I was just like such a pig, you know, like drink, drink, drink. The goal, of course, was to relieve that and then I guess, the goal after that anxiety was gone was just oblivion. Release from my life because I just didn't know how to cope with the stress of my life.

Towards the end of my drinking, certainly in the last year, my behaviour became very unpredictable. I think at home it was more predictable. When I was drunk, I remember being very, very fuelled by resentments and it was just this whole tape that would be playing in my mind of resentments. I would always have some resentments going that I would be focusing my energy on. Whether it would be my husband or families or friends or whatever. There was always someone or some colleagues at work. I had really irrational resentments, like some were probably justified but they took over my mind when I was drunk. I went into the fury of the drinking. Having this righteous anger and you know it would be part of the drinking experience. My expectations that I had that people should behave in certain ways or do certain things, were just fucking irrational. That was where my mind was at when I drank.

When I went out to drink I was much more unpredictable, it was like a roll of the dice. My last twenty-four hours of drinking I was actually out of the house. It was pretty blurry to be honest, but I know that there was great humiliation attached to it. I really behaved badly. I was probably, like kissing strangers, taking off my clothes, crying in the bathroom, falling over, just starting drama. It was the worst drunk nightmare. It was a shit show. I'm pretty sure my last drink was with work people. It was pretty fucked up and I remember the next day being horrified. I was not able to piece stuff together, but I had bits of memory. This was just one of the many times I behaved badly. That last night of drinking I had to deal with it, I was covered in bruises. I didn't really know what had happened and I'm just suspecting I had been falling over everywhere.

Basically, there's a few reasons that I got sober and not all of it was up to me. I was so sick that I think I had alcohol poisoning. I couldn't drink because I was violently ill and so I spent the next two days in bed. I was vomiting and shaking and crying uncontrollably for hours. I felt like I had this spiritual break. I actually reached this point of despair that I'd never had before.

Today I understand it was alcoholic despair, and I was incapable of the next thought. Two days went by and I was just in bed crying and throwing up and then on the third day in the morning, my husband got me out of bed. He put me in the shower and he was really angry with me, and he said "Just get you're fucking act together. Get dressed and go to work, or else you're going to lose your job." So I got up and got dressed but I couldn't function. It's still blows my mind I put on a fucking pants suit, I looked like Hillary Clinton, you know, going to work.

I got to work, walked in the front door of the building and had a complete panic attack. My boss could see what a mess I was in and she took me to the Medical Centre. I saw a GP and begged her to help me. She made a decision to send me to detox. She made the referral and sent me in a taxi to HADS. That decision changed my life. It was just one of those things that I can't believe. Other doctors would have sent me to a psych ward because of the state that I was in. I was clearly someone that was having a mental breakdown.

I'm grateful she thought that I was an alcoholic and that was the problem that needed to be addressed before my mental health, you know, as well as my mental health, obviously, but some other doctors might have sent me to the psych ward instead of the detox unit. While I was in detox, somebody came in from AA and talked about how they hadn't had alcohol for years, and that they had been able to get clean and sober by going to meetings and getting support. There was also an AA meeting list in there, so I took a meeting list but I didn't really know anything about recovery and I didn't know whether it would work. I just didn't understand anything, I was so clueless.

After I left the detox I think I started going to meetings pretty quickly because I was finding it so hard to stay sober. I did so much of my drinking at home. My house was full of triggers, and my husband also drank. So it wasn't actually a safe environment for me. He didn't understand my journey. He just wanted me to get my act together. I don't think he ever thought that I would stop drinking. He just needed me to stop having a fucking mental breakdown.

Being at home at the end of the day was really hard for me when I got sober, when the anxiety would build up in the afternoons. Once I started going to meetings, that really helped me so much because I knew if I could get through a couple of hours and then get to a meeting, something would happen in that meeting and I'd settle down. It would actually ease my anxiety because I could get out of the house and away from all of the triggers. The meetings would help me to remember the bigger picture of the change I was trying to make in my life.

I learned so much in the meetings. I heard people describe alcoholism for the first time. People understood what I was going through. It was really encouraging, but outside of the meetings I didn't feel understood and that was difficult in the beginning of my sober life. People say "Thank God," but I actually thank that doctor, because she was the one that started my recovery and then the people in AA were the ones that were there at meetings to support me and help me to stay sober one day at a time.

That's really a powerful message, if you've never heard it before. It worked in my life. When I came to the meetings, people would tell me what I needed to do every day, because they understood that every day was difficult for me. There was no kind of minimising the problem. I felt like I was understood. People knew exactly how difficult each day was for me without a drink. But they also let me know that it gets easier over time and I held onto that hope. And they were right. It did get easier.

I remember the early meetings really fondly. There was a lot of laughter. It was shocking, but people were able to laugh at the terrible things that had happened to them and it made me realise that there was distance between them and their drinking. I didn't know what that was at the time, but it was really attractive. I now know that's recovery. It's very important once you recognise that there's distance between the tragedy and what's happening now, there's hope in that.

> **Kym** is a mother of two and works in higher education. She remains hopeful for the future and continues to support others in their recovery journey.

17

Gail

It's a challenge to remember that final week of my drinking, it's all a bit of a blur. I was never the best witness to my drinking anyway. In that last week of drinking I knew I was going into rehab, so I went pretty hard. It was going to be, hopefully, the end of my drinking, so I did everything I could to drink to excess.

I still managed to look like I had it all together, but all I would do essentially was go to work, go home, feed my daughter, hope I could get her to sleep early, and then drink hard. I would wake up in the morning and survey the damage, which could be anything from mess everywhere, to a broken finger or bruise somewhere, maybe a broken electrical appliance or the phone in the dishwasher. Then there was the forensic analysis of the phone in the morning to find out who I had called and what I had done.

That was the nature of my drinking; I drank to oblivion.

My very last evening though was one of fear knowing I was going to rehab the next day and wanting to have my very last drink. I had to be there at nine the next morning and because nobody knew about my drinking, I was dependent on myself to get there, so I couldn't go too hard. There was already a sense of withdrawal and of mourning the loss of drinking, even before I'd stopped. I drank enough to get myself to sleep that night. My last evening was not one of rock bottom or one of mass destruction, but one of still needing to drink for relief.

I was in rehab for three weeks. I was hopeful of success, but I had already tried AA and that hadn't worked for me. I hadn't surrendered to the program in previous attempts, and I realised I had to do that if I wanted to get sober. I had absolutely no power over alcohol by this stage and nothing I saw or heard could stop me from going to the bottle shop. I knew I had to remove myself from that situation and rehab seemed my only hope. I was still quite delusional and thought I could get it in a week rather than the three weeks they suggested. I felt I could get the quick fix. I was used to doing everything at a fast pace, and it was challenging and scary to do otherwise. I wasn't used to being told what to do, I hadn't exactly been a team player in the past.

We were put into groups and I found listening to people and having a structured program a real challenge. I was also mourning the loss of what I thought was my best friend and saviour, alcohol. Having a good look at myself at that time was extremely difficult. Some of the staff were great and some not so good. There was a surprising amount of casual staff given that it was a private rehab, and my expectations had been of luxury, comfort and support, like the rest of my life was. I lived the high life and one of luxury, so it was a shock when I went in there and found myself sharing a room with three other people. They monitored me at first and then after a week I got my own room. That reality check was necessary and I was exactly where I needed to be.

I'd been in AA for two years by then, always in and out trying to get it. Having the desire to get sober but not the willingness. I didn't want to make myself that vulnerable. I was so used to fighting and of even fighting with myself. I just couldn't surrender. My ego was so huge at that stage that I couldn't be vulnerable enough to say to myself, "I need help." That's exactly what AA is, help and support through members sharing their experience, strength and hope with each other. I didn't want to tell anyone anything.

I was able to hide my drinking from pretty much everyone and drank without almost anyone knowing, I even tried to hide it from my partner. Both of us travelled with work a lot and I was overseas for six months of the year. My daughter was young and unaware of it. On odd occasions people would see me drunk or could tell that I'd had too much, but nobody knew I had a drinking problem as such. My life looked perfect from the outside.

I realised the last week of rehab was crucial for me in my recovery and I finally took things really seriously. A lot of people were mucking around, or leaving the rehab to drink, and I got very cranky over it. I became quite aggressive with people who weren't taking it seriously and I quickly became the Boss Lady. The nurses gave me the 'wooden spoon' as they called it, and I was in charge of getting everyone to group. I made enemies of people who weren't on time.

I think in those three weeks of detox I finally got to understand the real basis of AA. People from AA came to the rehab to speak throughout my time there and I had already listened to a few, but one beautiful old gentleman came in at the end of the last week and really made an impression on me.

With only two days to go I was becoming fearful of losing the safety that the rehab gave me. When this gentle old man in his late seventies came into share I had no expectations of him and really just thought, "Here we go again!" What transpired was the complete opposite. I related to him in a way I hadn't related to anyone else in AA.

I'm sure if I had been willing in the past I would have, but at that point I was so scared of going back out there and being powerless again over alcohol, and so I listened to that man and he really told my story. When the pupil is ready, the teacher appears ...

I hung around after he spoke instead of leaving straight away like I normally did. I actually asked him questions and he was a remarkable man. He was peaceful, calm and serene, like you think a sober older member should be. I really wanted what he had.

He asked me to go to his AA home group and I went the day after I left rehab. He asked me to be the 'greeting person' who met people at the door. He was like a gentle old grandfather to me and I didn't want to disappoint him so I agreed. That simple task of going there each week and greeting people, and the responsibility it entailed, kept me sober for my first twelve months. I didn't want to disappoint him and I knew I had to rock up there and be honest. That gave me some consistency in the program. It didn't initially give me a good quality of recovery by any means, but at least I stayed sober.

Then after a few years of being sober in AA without doing the suggested things, I hit a real rock bottom when I was living in England. I thought I was having a nervous breakdown. I had been collecting phone numbers over the years, but still hadn't reached out and called anyone, that's how big my ego still was.

When I hit that low I finally called someone in Sydney from London and said I really needed help as I wasn't coping. I needed to be vulnerable enough to say I needed help. So I asked, "What do I need to do? I no longer drink but I'm not relieving my head and heart and I need to live." We agreed I should return to Sydney and start 'working the program'.

It was nine years ago yesterday that I walked into that rehab and it was the last person I ever thought I could relate to who was the one who helped me the most. I know that now in hindsight, but at the time when I saw a man in his seventies or eighties, I thought; "This is an hour of my life I'll never get back!" Instead he gave me my whole life back.

> **Gail** lives on the Northern Beaches of Sydney and has been sober for nine years now, after spending her first two years in AA continually relapsing.

18

Brendan C

I vividly remember the last week of my drinking. The first time I drank I got drunk. I was ten years old and, in retrospect, I believe I was an alcoholic on day one, I believe I was born an alcoholic. I always loved drinking and getting drunk and partying. I never thought I was alcoholic but always loved what alcohol did to me.

I was thirty-nine when I stopped drinking. I'm a Jazz musician and that's all I've ever done, I'm a professional musician. It suited my lifestyle to drink and party and stay out all night. I've never really had a day job. I slept all day until I was thirty-two, until my daughter was born. I now do a bit of teaching at university.

By the time I was sixteen or seventeen I wasn't drinking every day of the week, but I was drinking most weekends with friends. I grew up in Canberra and we would sit in the reserve and get pissed, or if parents were away we would have a party. From seventeen, I would go to pubs and alcohol was easy to get. From eighteen I was a daily drinker and I was getting drunk every night. By the time I stopped, most of my drinking was happening on my own at home.

During the last year of my drinking, on one level I knew the game was up. It wasn't fun and I wasn't partying. I was a dad and I was married and my wife was saying "I think you have a problem" and I just would shut her down and say "Nah, I'm not talking about that." This was because admitting I had a problem was out of the question and unacceptable to me, and stopping drinking was totally out of the question.

I could not face up to that, because if I admitted to having a problem, it would be like a house of cards. Little did I know the greatest thing I ever did was to admit that I had a problem.

The thing was when I drank I couldn't guarantee my behaviour. I hated the person I was. I looked in the mirror and hated what I had become. I had let myself down so many times and I was doing things I wouldn't do when I wasn't drinking. I would let my family down. I would promise my wife I would be home by a certain time.

My wife was cool, she would say "Can you be home by 3:00 am?" That's pretty good but I couldn't manage it. I couldn't and wouldn't stop. I was thirty-nine and remember thinking "Maybe when I turn fifty I'll be able to have just a couple glasses of wine." I didn't think maybe when I turned forty. I was thinking ten years ahead, a buffer to allow me to drink for ten more years. It's amazing when you read AA's Big Book that people talk about the delusion that we will be able to drink like other people. That was definitely in my head. I just didn't have a stop button when it came to drinking alcohol. Also, I had no concept of the disease of alcoholism.

Fast forward to the last week of my drinking, I remember it really well. I had just completed a Master's Degree at the Sydney Conservatorium and was graduating. It was a miracle I had managed to complete that degree while I was drinking. I had a rule that I wasn't allowed to work on my Master's at night because that is when I drank. That actually worked, the one time I did drink and worked on my Master's I didn't save it and I lost a whole chapter of work so thought "I'd better not do that again." I would delay my drinking until the night.

A few months before this I had confided in a mate that I thought I had a drinking problem. He had been sober in AA for five years and I saw how AA had changed and transformed him. He was visiting from New Zealand and recommended I go to a meeting. I didn't go to AA but I managed to stop drinking for six weeks. It was hell, and I started drinking again and felt I went up another level.

I started drinking more secretly, drinking in the car. I started drinking spirits which I had avoided because I thought it was smart to only drink beer and wine. I discovered spiced rum and it was ridiculous, I never drank rum, but I thought spiced rum was fantastic. I was becoming more secretive and more desperate because my hangovers were getting worse and I was having severe anxiety and electric fleas. These things had never happened before, and I was getting scared.

That last week I was on an epic bender. I can't remember what I was doing early in the week but for three nights I got really hammered. My five year old daughter was doing a ballet concert and I went and had an epic anxiety attack and it really freaked me out. I thought I was having a heart attack and thought I would have to leave.

My last drink was on Sunday 14 December 2014 and the night before we had my in-laws over for a celebratory dinner, that was my last 'drunk'. My father in-law and I would often get on the piss together and that night was big. I remember at this point of my drinking not looking forward to getting pissed. I knew they were coming over though, and I felt sick and was dreading it because I'd been on a bender for three days, but there was no question that I had to get drunk. There's the powerlessness right there!

I was not looking forward to it so I smoked some weed and got 'off my face'. I got really drunk and the next day I was so sick, hungover, and anxious. I was spent and tired, and I had a gig that night and at the gig I had a beer, I would usually buy a six-pack. I didn't think a six-pack was drinking. To a non-alcoholic, a six-pack would be a lot to drink, but not to me.

My last drink, I had an afternoon gig and I was feeling anxious and sick and afraid. I did the gig and had a beer and I didn't enjoy it. I got home and had beers in the fridge, not my usual high alcoholic beer, and I got a beer and sat down. I don't think I drank the whole thing, I just looked at it thinking "I'm not enjoying this at all." I knew I was at the end and I don't remember if I finished it. I probably threw it out and that's the last drink I had.

And the next couple days I was spinning out and two days later I was having a mega anxiety attack and my wife took me to the doctor. I told him what was going on and I expected to get tests done and thought they would tell me I had cancer. My wife actually said "He's an alcoholic" and I thought "Oh God, that's the truth of it!" That's the day I went to my first AA meeting at the Crib in Newtown and that Sunday was the last day I drank alcohol.

I remember that first meeting really well, it was in this really old church in Newtown. I was nervous and drove around the block a few times. There were all these dudes standing out the front and they had tattoos and I thought "I'm not going to fit in here." When I walked up, one of those dudes put out his hand and said "G'day mate," told me his name and said "Come in" and a few people came up to me and said "G'day" and introduced themselves. It was an identification (ID) meeting, and I just knew I was in the right place.

I was asked to share a bit about my drinking story, which I did. After the meeting another dude came up and said I should buy a Big Book. A funny thing is I remember the guy who chaired that first meeting, and I saw him a few months ago. That's really weird, how many meetings do you go to and remember who was in the chair?

> **Brendan C.** is a professional musician and was for many years a professional drunk. He has been sober in AA for over seven years, one day at a time, and will always be eternally grateful for the new life that AA has given him.

19

Val C

I first came into Alcoholics Anonymous in January 2018 after disclosing my problems to a member and they said to me, "You know, let's go to a meeting" and I thought that might be a fun idea on a Tuesday night. I'd only had a couple of drinks. I was about to lose my house and my job. I had around $30,000 debt, and thought I was pretty much a lost case. Little did I know I had to hit a bigger 'rock bottom' before I actually started to recover.

That first meeting was on the Sydney North Shore and I didn't understand anything that was written on the banners, and when they read out Chapter 5, I felt like it went for five hours. But for the first time in my life, I felt like I was home. I'd never really considered AA before even though my mother had been in AA for six months. I've got so many family members that are alcoholics we could have our own closed AA meeting. AA was never an option for me, but I knew I was crossing some 'thin red lines' and 'red flags' were coming up left, right and centre. Not enough for me to stop drinking though, I thought I was born with a ticket to drink. I thought I was meant to drink for the rest of my life.

The last day of my drinking was the 27th March 2020. I bought a bottle of Gin and a case of mixers and drank myself stupid, and I was ready to take some pretty high-dose prescription medicines. I remember sitting out the back on the patio, thinking "I don't enjoy the feeling of being drunk as much as I thought I did." It was really strange.

I had my first drink at the age of eight. It was half a bottle of wine with my brother and his friends. I watched my mother drink to blackout in the clubs very close to our house so when I started drinking it was 'monkey see, monkey do' and I thought it was normal. I started drinking alcoholically as a teenager, getting insanely drunk on weekends, or any opportunity I could. That I could drink as much as I wanted without stopping was exciting. In early adulthood my drinking really took off. Occasionally I went out with people but I mostly drank alone in isolation. I used alcohol to cope with things in my life, you know, situations. I loved being able to black myself out from reality and set out to do that every time I drank.

I've had two careers, the first was in Optometry. I was living alone in a unit in the Eastern Suburbs and drinking daily. If there was a work function or opportunity to go out and drink, I was always the one that went too far. I don't remember one work function that ended well. As time went on I drank more and more, and the more I drank the worse my problems got, the smaller my social circle got, and the further downhill my mental health went. In AA I've heard about alcoholism being a progressive disease and this seems true for me.

Despite that I thought drinking was fantastic, "I'm living by myself, I can drink as much as I want, when I want and nobody can tell me otherwise." But, the circle was getting smaller and people didn't want to drink with me, or if they did they'd make their exit plan and leave. Or I would only stay a few hours and leave, saying I was tired. There was a bottle shop downstairs from my unit and I lied to myself "My own four walls would protect me" and it was obviously cheaper to drink alone.

Anyway, I'd had a few months off work and went into my second career, the finance industry. It was acceptable to drink on a Monday, at lunchtime, or after work. In the last six months, I'd sustained a back injury. I'd fallen onto the tiles in my kitchen in a blackout and woken up with a black eye and a sore back with no recollection of what had happened. That was just one red flag, but it didn't stop my drinking.

By the end of 2019 things were serious. I was turning up to work hungover every single day and struggling to do my job. I was having multiple panic attacks and mental breakdowns. I'd actually gone to a work Christmas party, had cocaine with me and was drinking. I had a blackout and was put in a taxi home. A few weeks later, I was going to suicide so some colleagues took me to a friend's place for a get-a-way. That ended in a three day bender and getting a police caution for drugs, and being drunk and disorderly in The Rocks. I didn't realise until I was in AA, but I was at my absolute 'rock bottom'. I was on the near edge of death.

I was fifty-two days sober before I had my last drink. We had gone into COVID-19 lockdown and told to work from home. I was working with a colleague from home, and had thrown the idea of AA out the door. I flipped from being someone willing and ready to jump into the AA program, to someone who let go of AA and ran on 'self will'. In AA they talk about 'yet', and one of the things I had 'yet' to do was drink a martini while working, and that thought went through my brain. So, I picked up one martini and a few days later I was back to my old way of drinking.

My drinking wasn't extravagant, I wasn't one who partied. Occasionally I would go out but I was mainly at home alone and isolated. When I stopped drinking previously, I was drinking two bottles of wine a day and a bottle of Jack Daniels, alone. I went straight back to that.

Being in AA for those couple of months changed my perspective, I felt a lot of guilt and shame. I found out a longtime friend of mine was in AA and admitted to them I was drinking. I kept drinking for a few days and on my way to the medicine cabinet I got a text message which could very well have saved my life. It was from that very friend who was sober in AA "How was your day?"

The next day I went into the city, in the middle of the lockdown. No one was around except for the homeless man on the park bench at Circular Quay. I looked up to the sky and said, "God, I can't do this anymore. I cannot do this any more." I knew even in that short bender, about a week, I was straight back to old habits, old ways of thinking, and burning bridges. I was getting in contact with people that I didn't want to be in contact with, and I felt so alone. I felt really ashamed and felt I'd failed myself and had let a lot of people down. That friend of mine kindly 'carried me back into AA' with my tail between my legs.

It took a couple of weeks to identify with the stories. I was back to counting the days. That last drink highlighted where I'll end up if I drink again. I liken it to touching a stove to see if it's hot. When I touched that stove I'm really lucky I didn't cause a more serious burn.

I realise I made a conscious decision to pick up that first drink. I believe the disease of alcoholism overpowered my brain "You'll be alright if you just have one" but that 'one' went on for multiple days. It turned into distress and ultimately me wanting to kill myself. I no longer wanted to live with myself or with decisions I had made, knowing the track that I was going down.

I came into the rooms mid-January 2020 and that's when my AA journey started. I describe my life now as being completely changed. A complete 180 from the life that I was living, it's not perfect, but today I'm able to get through life, one day at a time, without picking up a drink. I don't wake up anymore thinking about suicide or going through my day thinking about wanting to die. I'm able to get up today and be a successful person. I still have that job I nearly lost. I've been promoted three times and I'm now a senior leader in that business.

I rent a beautiful house on the North Shore, I pay my bills on time and have more beautiful friends, in and out of recovery, than I can poke a stick at. In my drinking, I didn't have anyone and struggled to make friends. The main difference in my life today is that I've got my mental health back. I was at the point where I thought my brain was about to stop. I've got sanity and peace of mind today, and I'm able to live a life that I never dreamed of. I'm able to achieve things and feel good about it.

At the end of my drinking, there was no light at the end of the tunnel. I couldn't see any future. I knew there was something inside me wanting to come out. Alcohol had pushed it down for so many years. Alcohol was the number one decision maker.

Today, I really enjoy the life I have. I'm able to deal with life as a sober person, which is something I haven't experienced before. There's so many future prospects that I look forward to.

Val is twenty-two years old and two years sober.

20

Jake W

I always feel that the story of my last week of drinking isn't particularly spectacular or interesting really. By the time I had the last week of my drinking I had been trying to stop for about three years. I had my first experience of sobriety in 2001. My vanity got the better of me and one morning I was so scared of my ageing appearance in the mirror that I stopped drinking for a year and a half. Never mind that I could have lost my life the night before, the thing that really scared me was my appearance.

During that period of time I wasn't a member of any Twelve Step fellowship. The closest I came was working for a staging and events company in Sydney where there was a guy called Sven who worked for the company. Sven was clean and sober in AA and was always talking about this other workmate who was a really angry guy and always losing his rag. Sven would say the workmate doesn't have a Higher Power and weird spiritual stuff like that which I thought was kookie, but I did have to admit Sven was always happy-go-lucky and unfazed.

I think Sven mentioned he was also in NA and I told him I wasn't drinking. In my arrogant head I thought "I've solved this drinking thing, I'm not drinking anymore and all I need to do is to look in the mirror and realise I'm getting old too fast." But for whatever reason I guess what had happened was a miraculous thing because, for years before that, I had never been able to go for more than a week without drinking.

A little later that same company said that we had a job for the 2002

AA National Convention, where we needed to build some stages and put some drapery inside the Sydney Town Hall. The job manager, who was a screaming alcoholic, took us aside and cautioned, "Just keep in mind these clients are actual alcoholics. They are not people working *for* alcoholics but real alcoholics." I didn't take too much notice and walked into the Town Hall to do the job. There were AA banners and signs all around the walls, including the Twelve Steps.

I had always expected the twelve steps would go something like "Stop drinking." I knew the first step was that you have to admit you're an alcoholic and stop drinking but I thought it would then go something like "Get a haircut, get a gym membership, get a job." But it was all very spiritual and the "God" word was mentioned all over the place; I sort of flipped out over all this and thought, "It's a kind of religious cult."

Then I thought "Isn't it great, I've managed to stop drinking and I didn't need any of this. I've managed to do it all on my own!" That's really what I thought and I was sure I would never drink again because my life was so improved by not drinking. I thought there was no way I would go back to the way it was when I was drinking.

I didn't have anyone in my life who was on the same journey though. I was pretty well living my life the same way that I did when I was drinking, except without the alcohol. I had no way of moving forward, but I thought I could maintain this new status quo.

Then one morning I was crossing King Street in Newtown on a pedestrian crossing when a car nearly ran into me and I saw it was an ex-girlfriend who had broken my heart years before. For years I had used that breakup as an excuse to get drunk. She had been the true love of my life, but I knew I had behaved appallingly in that relationship and that any sane person would have left me too.

She had moved to Sydney and we wound up getting back together. The pressures and jealousies returned, all the stuff I had been living without. As soon as our romance started up again, I reverted to type turning back into this scared, jealous, paranoid, needy person;

and then the drinking wasn't far behind. Once I was back in that emotional state, I couldn't cope. The only tool in the shed was booze and I started drinking again. She left me again, good on her (laugh). She's the only person I've made amends to who didn't take it well. Good on her! We still don't speak.

So then I was back drinking but I thought "I'll do what I did before and look in the mirror and think about my future, and I just won't drink." I think I might have managed a week, then I managed two weeks, then it was a day and I went on for a whole year like that, desperately trying to stay stopped. I had stopped for a month when I was living in Germany but I always started again.

I had an old friend from New Zealand and we had been drinking together since 1990. We had been living in a share-house and at nineteen years of age we would have conversations about whether it was the third or fourth drink that meant you had to keep drinking. He had moved to Sydney in 2002 and we were up to our old antics. Every time I had a drink for whatever reason, the consequences of what was going to happen if I picked up a drink weren't in my mind, they were always there though when I decided to put down the drink. The mysterious thing was there was no connection, no reconciling those polarities.

We had a mutual friend he was romantically interested in and I knew he would not listen to me because we drank the same, so I thought "I'll tell her that he is an alcoholic and she will tell him to go to AA." I hadn't actually done the calculations in my head but what happened was he went to AA and I managed to go too because I had someone to hold my hand when I went to my first meeting. He only stayed sober a couple of years but for whatever reason I kept going.

I'm unsure about the timeline but the last two drinks I had were on a Wednesday night at Beach Road Hotel at Bondi. Some friends of mine were in a Melbourne based band. They had a gig and I went and got drunk.

Something strange had happened with my drinking since that period of abstinence, something new had crept in. If I had a blackout and had possibly done something terrible, I used to feel guilt, shame and remorse. Now, I would feel guilt, shame and remorse without having a blackout, calamity and whatever else went on.

On rare occasions I could go out without any drama happening. That used to be my ideal. A successful night's drinking was to drink as much as I wanted without the blackouts, the personality change, and without abusing someone. I thought if I could do that I would feel alright inside and I wouldn't have the crippling dread and all the rest of it.

That night in Bondi I didn't blackout and got home. I woke up the next morning and felt like shit and felt empty inside, it was like my soul had been damaged. It was more than physical, like my actual soul and the good person I felt I was seemed to be disappearing. I was losing myself somehow.

Two nights later I went to Newcastle to see the band play again. A small gig, three people and a dog. I told them "I'm not going to be drinking so I can drive the van back and they agreed." I went to the gig and I got bored and my future romantic partner didn't seem to be there. So, after ten minutes, I went to the bar and started drinking. After the gig I asked for the band to keep playing because I was never satisfied for a night to come to an end. But they didn't want to kick on, so I had more drinks and that unspectacular event turned out to be the occasion of my last drink, which was nineteen years ago now.

I think there was this little part of me that wanted to survive. This tiny part of me that wanted another life and I knew that I couldn't have that life if alcohol was in it. Sober alcoholics talk about 'clarity' but I think it was 'vanity' with me and I don't understand why I was given this gift and others haven't.

From my experience if people don't have that internal rearrangement then everything is tenuous. They can stop drinking but it's tenuous.

The head can still tell you it's ok to drink. When I first went to meetings I was never equal to others. I was always 'worse than' or 'better than', thankfully AA has taught me to see otherwise.

I went to regular lunchtime meetings and met some amazing people and found hope in the rooms from people who had been sober for decades as well as brand spanking new members. The conditions were right for me getting into the rooms of AA. I went to different types of meetings all over Sydney and it's paid off.

Jake is a painter.

21

Rosemary L

I remember stealing alcoholic drinks (cocktail liqueurs) from my parent's pantry in my early teens, but don't remember getting drunk. When I was twelve or thirteen I went to a club in Surfers Paradise with my parents and there was a cute drummer in the band. He knew my father and he sat next to me and although I was under age, I looked eighteen. He slipped me a Bourbon and I remember feeling giddy. Nothing else happened but on the way home I threw up on myself in the car and I told my parents he gave me a drink and they were furious.

Then, when I was fifteen, I drank again while staying with an older friend on the Gold Coast. We regularly went to a nightclub in Coolangatta, 'The Patch', and I would drink port and lemonade as it was cheap and I always got drunk. It just went on from there around the pubs in Brisbane. I remember that drinking two or three drinks was my limit but every now and then that didn't work and I would get really drunk. I never saw it as a problem. I was disappointed that people could drink more than me.

I had an alcoholic father but never imagined I had inherited the same disease. I didn't drink often but when I did it only took a small amount and I was drunk. I stopped drinking when I was twenty-six and expecting my first child. I didn't drink for many years after that, fearful of the consequences. However, after the breakdown of my first marriage, I found alcohol again and made up for lost time! I eventually began drinking daily, a glass of wine while I cooked dinner, that ended in an empty bottle or two by bedtime.

I never got into trouble drinking alcohol. My behaviour was more of the same, just louder and more in your face. Not aggressive or augmentative like my father. I was proud that I wasn't like him. Then I started having blackouts where I would go out drinking, and the next day there would be gaps in my memory of the whole night. One night I went to an engagement party with friends where I drank a lot and couldn't remember paying for my dinner. It was at a restaurant and we paid for our own dinner and I woke up horrified that I had forgotten to pay. So I rang my friend and he said "No, we paid together, remember?" I still couldn't remember and that worried me.

I did take some risks when I drank, particularly with men, and became disinhibited as a result of alcohol. I was lucky to avoid catching an STI or getting bashed. That behaviour was a bit scary and it worried me, but not enough to consider stopping drinking. Stephen was a one night stand, or so I thought. He asked for my number and walked me home the next morning. Lucky for me he was a keeper and so I didn't go out drinking without him much after we met. We met in a pub when we were both drunk and we continued to go to pubs most weekends to listen to music, always leaving drunk. We married two years later.

I came into AA after a weekend of heavy drinking. I can't remember the details but Stephen and I had been out drinking on Saturday night. I noticed that early on Sunday he started drinking again and passed out and I thought "That's odd." Then he got up and started drinking again. I tended not to drink during the day and waited for the afternoon to continue drinking.

On Monday he rang me at work and said he had something to tell me. He had been to an AA meeting. We had only been married six months so I said we would talk about it at home. I remember thinking "Oh! What will I do? Who will I drink with now?" then "Maybe I drink too much. Maybe I should go to AA too." My main concern was that I couldn't imagine drinking if he wasn't. Something in me felt that it would mean the end of our marriage even though we didn't drink the same alcohol. I felt that I couldn't drink if he was going to be sober.

It dawned on me that I should be supportive. He drank a lot more than me and although he had been in AA before, he never told me before we married. I remember saying to him "You can put it away!" and he said "I've always been a heavy drinker and I have no intention of stopping." I replied, "I'm not asking you to stop, I'm just making an observation."

I was meeting an old friend who was in AA the next day for coffee and thought I should talk to her about it. I broached it with her and she responded with "I'm going to a meeting tonight. Why don't you come and see what it's all about? You don't have to join or sign up and you can make your own mind up about it." I figured I didn't have anything to lose and everything to gain so I picked her up on the way to the meeting that night.

I don't know what it was but something happened in that room and I just knew I was going to have this journey where I no longer drank. I never had trouble going without alcohol for periods of time but once I had a drink, all bets were off. If I had a drink I couldn't stop and although I didn't drink much compared to some, it was too much for me and I got drunk very quickly.

At the AA meeting, I remember that there was a feeling of peace and the people who talked were talking about a sense of hope or something like that. Some of these people had been hopeless alcoholics and were now leading positive lives and they didn't need to drink. There was a young girl that had been in AA a long time. She got in aged seventeen, and although she didn't come from an alcoholic home she had low self-esteem. She drank on weekends and her story resonated with me and I thought "Oh there are other people like me." That had a big impact on me.

At that point I didn't know about the Big Book or the Steps but somebody came up to me and said "There's another meeting on Thursday night at Mt Gravatt." I did go to that meeting and the interesting thing is this girl never came near me. I thought that was odd, that she had asked me to come to the meeting and didn't come near me but that was twelve years ago. Sponsorship helped me too.

My sponsor understood what was going on in my head as he had similar experiences.

As Stephen worked nights and I worked days and as our relationship was based around drinking, I was concerned that we might not last the distance once alcohol was out of the picture. Thankfully, that was not the case. We have both been sober twelve years, one day at a time.

Stephen had periods of sobriety in AA but he had never told me about it. He realised that if he didn't stop drinking, it would affect our marriage. That was very powerful for me as I thought "He really thinks I'm worth it." I never felt like anyone considered me worth the effort until that moment. I mean, my first husband was considerate in the beginning but it didn't last once we had kids due to the stress, so we went our own way. Stephen was more attentive without smothering me.

I was very sensitive to alcohol but it never stopped me from drinking it until I made that connection in the AA meetings. It was a revelation to me that it was a disease, not a flaw in my character. I had a bookshelf of self-help books, had attended personal development courses, but nothing seemed to help until I started working with a sponsor and the Twelve Steps. I learnt that I wasn't a bad person trying to get good, I was a sick person trying to get well. Taking responsibility for my behaviour and owning my character defects has freed me from self-pity and blame and made me a more compassionate and less judgemental human being. I am so grateful to the AA fellowship for the path I was steered towards and I will continue to practise the principles in all my affairs. Progress not perfection is my motto these days.

> **Rosemary** got sober at the age of 51 and at time of writing is 64. She works in a large Public Hospital as a Switchboard Operator and has three adult sons, two grandchildren, a step daughter and three step grandchildren. Her passions are needlework, quilting and travel.

22

Robbie Dunn

I came home from the Cleveland RSL club where I had the catering contract, it was a quiet night so I had spent half of it at the bar. The thing about blackouts is you cannot, for obvious reasons, remember them either from drinking alcohol or emotional and mental disorders. I suffered both, what a terrible concoction and trying to apologise for something you can only remember bits of is just about impossible. The members in the RSL club had been really great to me in helping me settle when I came to Queensland, Oz. They gave me furniture, beds and kitchenware and one of the members sold me a twenty-year-old Volkswagen that had belonged to his wife who had died.

Cooking was, and still is, my passion and the members appreciated my cuisine. In Dublin and London, I had worked with some of the best chefs in the world, training in French and Italian cuisine with sauces as my special passion. I always swore I would never drink once I put my chef's uniform on as I had a bad experience when I was seventeen, and I stuck by that rule until I was thirty-three years of age. However alcohol is such a mind-bending drug that rule slowly went by the wayside, customers would buy me a beer in the club in the morning or at lunch time and of course I would say yes because the addiction was getting worse, and off I would go again.

I was on an emotional roller-coaster. I could run a big business successfully, in fact like a clock, and never get a complaint, but put me in an emotional situation and I was unable to handle it. I was a reactor, so when my brother-in-law was found robbed and dead in his car in 1984, I was devastated. I wrote a song called "Tomorrow is Too Late," and every time I drank, I'd start crying over Jim - I loved him so much.

I was lying on a beach in Spain in 1984 – my father, brother and I had travelled there to drown our sorrows after Jim's untimely death. I had brought the guitar and took to doing gigs in the bars and we paid for nothing. I looked up one evening and there were twenty-seven bottles of wine and champagne on our table. The manager of the hotel wanted me to stay and offered me a deal but even then, I realised I would drink myself to death if I stayed. I was also offered gigs in Germany, but again I knew I would be in big trouble if I went there. Lying on this Spanish beach I thought "I am going to go to Australia, I have to get away from this."

I had worked with a man named Kevin in the Clarence Hotel, Dublin. We were good friends, he was twenty-eight, a handsome man with blond hair who worked as a kitchen porter. I walked into the staff hall one day and he was crying, a letter in his hand. I asked what was wrong, he said "My brother in Perth, Australia, has an engineering company and wants me to go over, he has a job for me." I asked, "Why don't you go?" and he replied "I can't because of my drinking, I cannot stop." In my innocence I said to him "Just stop," he said "I can't." I didn't understand the power of addiction.

Later in Cleveland, my drinking was now out of control and the addiction got worse by the day, riding me to the graveyard, blackouts were now the norm. I would go into the cold-room to get something and stand there not able to remember what I went in for, the confusion of what was happening to me was horrendous, I was a mess and functioning by rote. I could not handle small tasks, everything was causing me stress and yet I had everything to live a happy life.

Unknown to me I was carrying the weights of childhood abuse in my head, the beatings by the Christian brothers along with psychological brainwashing, as well as beatings from my father. This, coupled with my addiction to alcohol, was dragging me down into the pits of hell. In my mind I felt everyone was attacking me, and the walls were closing in. The emptiness, the loneliness, the pain and confusion were getting worse, it was like trying to slay a ten-headed dragon I could not see. I would go running or swimming every day, do an hour in the gym, into the sauna then up to the pub. I could not see the madness of that.

In Ireland I would hide my car so my mates would not call in for me to go for a drink, I would say "Yes" when I wanted to say "No." "Come on grab the guitar" and we would go into the ballad pubs around Dublin; Tailors Hall, Temple bar or O'Donoghue's and the odd trip up the Dublin mountains to some little out of the way pub. We usually got free drinks, but as I know now, there is no such thing as a free drink, everything has a cost. How none of us were not killed, I will never know – drink driving is a bad idea.

I came home from the RSL club and had an argument with my wife and then exploded and punched the walls out. All the suppressed abuse took off like a rocket. I started to hate everyone and thought "If I could only get them out of my life everything would be fine." I terrified everyone, including my children whom I loved dearly and swore I would always protect after what had happened to me as a child. The nightmare was in full swing. My brain was in turmoil against my will, I was saying and doing things which made no sense to me.

The next day I headed for Sydney in the twenty-year-old Volkswagen, a thousand kilometre journey with a bottle of booze between my legs. My head was like a gothic merry-go-round being pulled around in circles, I could not get a handle on it, it was terrifying. The drive to Sydney was like the night terror I suffered as a child with big trucks coming up beside me or behind me, blowing their air horns. The fact that the wrong tyres were on the car did not help, each wheel wanted to go in a different direction, like trying to drive a car on tram tracks. I cannot remember much of the drive, I think someone or something else must have been guiding me because I was in no fit state to drive. I don't know if I did the drive in one hit or whether I stayed in a hotel on the way, all

I know is I drove to Sydney and stopped the car outside a pub on a corner and went in and had a few beers.

I had a phone number for Shae, someone I knew from the folk scene in Tailors Hall, Dublin. I met him through Liam Weldon, a famous Irish Seanchai. I went to the phone box outside the pub with my beer in one hand and a smoke in the other and rang him. After exchanging pleasantries, I said "It's Robbie Dunn here, I just drove down from Brisbane. I was wondering if you could put me up for the night." "No problem" he said, "Where are you now?" I said "Sydney." He said "Look, get on to William Street." I looked up at the street sign and it said "William Street!" He said "That's amazing you are only five minutes away from my place, it's Waratah Street" and gave me the address. "I'll be home later, see you then."

I went around, parked the car and like every good alcoholic headed for Kings Cross until Shea came home. I don't remember much of this but years later Shea very gently said to me, "You were very sick Robbie." I didn't know how sick I was and neither do most practising alcoholics. It's a disease and if you drink alcohol it only gets worse.

Shea brought the paper home and the next morning said there's a unit around the corner for $70 a week, so we rang about it, had a cup of coffee and left. Just as we were walking down the corridor his phone rang and he walked back to get it. "Oh hello Bridget, how are you going?" and related my story and she said "Well my lodger has just left I have a spare room bring him over here", so off we set. The house was in Chippendale on Cleveland Street. I moved in ... there was something very special about this house, Bridget was a very spiritual person, not religious but spiritual.

I managed to get my head together, control my drinking and got a job as the Head Chef in the American Express building in North Ryde and, of course, met up with some folkies around the scene. Bridget said to me after a few weeks "I've been here years and you know more people than I do!" I had to have a drink before I started work though and got stuck into the cask of white wine that I used for my sauces just to settle me down. I met Martin Docherty who had a band called Roisin, they were pretty big and played in the Rocks. I would get up and do a few songs and started getting little gigs around the place.

At this stage the night terrors were happening, there was evil all around me at night in my room. Shadowy figures and twisted spirits came out of the walls, terrifying me and leaving me frozen in my bed. The winds of the universe were now whipping through me, I was an empty vessel, knew death was coming, I could smell it. I was not in control, alcohol was. All I knew was I was in the horrors, most of the time my nervous system was shattered, I was the loneliest man in the world. I was so ashamed of my behaviour I couldn't even ring my children, I was in fact mortified.

I played a gig in an Irish bar and got talking to a woman afterwards. We walked the streets of Sydney, I said to her "I don't know what I am doing here, I don't know where I am going, I am totally lost" she felt the same way and showed me some well worn photographs of her children that she'd lost through alcoholism. I asked her to hold me, but couldn't get rid of the emptiness inside of me, it was horrific.

I thought the end was coming, little did I know it was going to get worse before it got better. No one can understand the depths of despair I was in, however, my real life was just about to begin.

Christmas Day came and went. I spent it at a house overlooking Sydney harbour and actually drank very little for some strange reason. I was booked to play in a pub on New Year's Eve in Chippendale and the festivities began early. As far as I know we had a great night, it was an out of my head night but I do remember parts of it. I was invited back to various houses but went off with a load of punk rockers that had adopted me. The next thing I remember I woke up around four am in a squat looking at the ceiling wondering "Where the fuck am I?"

My wallet was still in my pocket and my guitar was by my side and no one had knifed me. The weird thing was there was no one else there. I staggered out the door half crying and totally distraught. Walking up the street with my guitar over my shoulder I called out to Jim my brother-in-law who had died in '84, "For fuck's sake Jim I need help," a good Dublin man's prayer. I knew Jim loved me, he had told me before he died (maybe it was a premonition), I had no belief or understanding in any God or religion, it never made sense to me.

I made it home somehow to my room and went out cold and slept well. I woke up around 10:00 am and felt well rested, the first time in a long time. Made a coffee, tried to remember the night before – waking up around 4:00 am in the squat and calling out to Jim for help. I was in a really strange place in my head, I'd never asked anyone for help in my life, I saw it as a sign of weakness, but something had changed, that guiding force was pushing me along. I got the bright idea that I might try to stop drinking and sort out my life. Somehow or other I got the phone number for AA and rang but there was no answer; it was the 1st of January, 1987. I put down the phone and turned to iron a shirt. I was going to the pub so the stopping drinking idea was short lived.

With that, this guy Dave who was staying in the house and had just come out of rehab for Christmas came out of the bedroom with his girl friend Joanna. We got talking about drinking and I said to him "I hate it!" "Do you want to stop?" he asked and I said "I've stopped many times" and he said "The trick is to stay stopped," I agreed. " I'm going to a meeting tonight, would you like to come along?" Ever the people pleaser, I said "Ok" immediately thinking "Why did I say Ok?"

I put on my ironed shirt and said "I'm off to the pub for a beer. Do you want to come?" He was horrified, "But you said you wanted to stop" "I do but not yet." I headed out the door and he said "I'll go with you." Joanna said frantically "Are you sure Dave?" he said "I'll be Ok".

Up to the pub we went and people shouted out to me "Great night last night Robbie." I was about to order a beer when Dave jumped in and ordered two cokes. "Oh, fuck" I said, "Do we have to start straight away?" "Just don't have that one." I'd already had my last drink and didn't know it. I kept thinking "How do I get rid of him? Maybe I overreacted, maybe it wasn't that bad." I was in the horrors, my life was in bits, and this is what my head was saying to me.

Dave stuck to me like a limpet all day, made sure I didn't drink and filled me up with food. Before I knew it we were heading across the harbour bridge to the 7:30 pm meeting. I walked in and was immediately greeted by a man called Ron who stuck out his hand and said "My name is Ron, I am an alcoholic, welcome home. Would you like a cup of coffee?" I felt safe straight away then people started to arrive. I was introduced one by one, they were all really friendly and I noticed them hugging each other which was foreign to me.

The meeting progressed and I could not believe what they were saying, I had never heard such honesty in my life. They spoke of the loneliness, the pain and confusion of being an alcoholic. No more sitting in the Dublin mountains thinking "What the fuck is wrong with me." I was in the process of finding out, it was like I'd been guided to this moment and place. A little light came on inside me, a ray of hope. Ron was like an angel and said "If you are in any trouble just keep saying the Serenity Prayer, like a mantra until the crisis passes."

The next day I was walking up the street and the pub was on the corner two hundred metres away, I was terrified I would go in. I got out the prayer and continually said it, next thing I knew I was two hundred metres past the pub, a miracle!

I put my trusty Volkswagen on the train and headed back to Brisbane and what lay ahead. I was full of hope for the future but one thing I have learned is I am not in charge. I do not remember my last drink because I was out of my head.

I dedicate this story to the memories of all my friends, over thirty at the last count, who have died prematurely of mental illness, alcohol and child abuse, all common denominators.

Robbie is an Irish entertainer, poet, and songwriter.

23

Mike K

I had my first drink when I was ten. I stole two long neck beers out of the fridge, and I drank them beside the house at a family party. I threw up and went to bed. I remember a loss of coordination and I liked that feeling of being outside myself, feeling myself going numb and my head spinning. I didn't drink much again until I was about fourteen. Then it was on weekends and when I could manage to stay at other people's houses. My friends were all older than me. My best friend from childhood was sixteen and I mixed with his mates, and the girls they knew. I got lots of exposure to drinking and sexual activity with this older group. My drinking didn't cause any real problems until I was seventeen or eighteen when it started being linked with violence. Looking back now, it was my behaviour that caused most of the trouble.

I started my first job when I was seventeen, working in the basement of the old Brisbane Anzac Square building with a group of much older men. These blokes were all ex WWll servicemen, and most were big drinkers. Back then you were paid in cash and for a number of them, their wives would turn up on pay day and get the money because their husbands couldn't be trusted. If they got cash, they would head straight to the pub and drink it. Some of those blokes who didn't have access to alcohol for whatever reason would drink aftershave and methylated spirits, strangely, something I didn't think of as being all that odd at the time. There was a culture of drinking both inside and outside the workplace and 'why drink on your own time when you can drink on someone else's'.

By eighteen I was drinking heavily and it was accepted in both my work and social environments. There was no taboo around it. Everyone drank and I didn't associate with anyone who didn't drink. The only person who I knew who didn't drink was my mother. She had a bottle of gin that lasted her seven years.

I'm someone who should never have drunk alcohol, but the disease of alcoholism wants you to drink.

I had first gone to AA in September 1989 after a set of unfortunate incidents, but without any real intention of stopping drinking. I knew I should stop drinking but, at my first AA meeting when they told me it was "Just for today" I couldn't drink. I knew that this actually meant I had to stop long-term if I was to have any real chance. I identified as being alcoholic at my first meeting but stopping drinking was a bit much for a twenty-six year old, it was ok for all the 'old blokes' at the meeting (younger than I am now actually) but I was a young bloke and how could you seriously expect me to stop drinking, my life would be over. While my drinking and behaviour was out of control when I drank, it wasn't so bad as to have to stop completely.

I went to one AA meeting a week and managed to stay off the grog from September 1989 until I went on a work trip to north Queensland in February 1990. The first night away on the trip I stopped in Rockhampton and that's when I had my first drink since the previous September.

That first night away drink was a big drink and resulted in a blackout, but no serious incidents occurred. Just another blackout and waking up in the morning as sick as a dog. "So far so good" I thought, and all this AA stuff about staying away from the first drink was obviously rubbish. AA got the flick.

The next day I drove from Rockhampton to Mackay, booked into a pub, started drinking mid-afternoon and continued right through to the night. It was heavy drinking from the start but that was normal. It's important to recognise I didn't drink for enjoyment;

I drank to get drunk, to get to that feeling you get three-quarters of the way into a bottle of rum. If I could have just stayed there it would have been fine, but I could never stop drinking once I started. It was drink until blackout and then continue.

Partial blackout again although I remembered having dinner at the bar of the pub. The next thing I remember after that is coming to in a hospital bed. It was morning, I had been admitted after a violent altercation at the pub, police and ambulance had attended and multiple people were involved. I obviously came off second best and was taken to hospital. I spent that day in the hospital. A nurse told me what she knew of the incident, but I didn't remember what had actually happened other than snippets of a fight. The police wanted to speak to me, but a nurse and doctor had told them I wasn't well enough to be spoken to. The police left but said they would come back later to see me. As soon as I got the opportunity, I checked myself out of the hospital, went to the airport and got a ticket out. Back to Brisbane for me.

That proved to be my last drink. Waking up in that hospital bed was the first time I made any real connection between my drinking and what had happened, there being no-one else to blame but me. Prior to that it had always been someone else's fault, a set of circumstances, if he or she hadn't done this or that nothing would have happened. I was just a good bloke having a bad trot. However, laying in that hospital bed was the first time I linked it all together.

My drinking had caused the shit I was in, and it didn't have to be that way. It was so clear in my mind. Laying in that bed I remember thinking "What those old pricks in AA have been saying might be true." "If you're an alcoholic person and continue to drink things will just get bad, rotten and worse." Prior to that I thought they were old fools and giving up drinking was never going to happen. That morning in the hospital bed, however, I wanted to stop drinking and knew it was my only chance. I could just see things getting worse. The stories I heard in AA in the few months I had been going to meetings were about to come true for me, I could see it all played out in front of me. The stories I had listened to from men and women like Ross, Bob and Glenda had seen them transformed in my mind from stupid old pricks to people who may actually know what they were talking about. This change saved my life. In fact, it gave me a life.

Within a few days of getting back to Brisbane I went to the Thursday night AA meeting at Mt Gravatt with a swollen face and black eye. Bob saw me when I walked in and said something like "Looks like someone has had a bust" and he told me "That's what alcoholics do, the important thing is to get back to the meetings and get fair-dinkum about giving this a go." I knew AA was the only chance I had. The 6th of February 1990 was my last drink.

Because of my early return from the work trip, commitments that had been made had to be cancelled. The person I was travelling with had already informed my workplace of what had occurred while I was in hospital. This provided another black mark against my work performance which had been riddled with alcohol fueled incidents for some years. Although I didn't get sacked, I got moved from that job into a back-water type role and that was the end of it for a while. However, at the back of my mind I had this feeling of impending doom that my drinking had once again created a set of circumstances I could not overcome.

That feeling of impending doom realised itself a few months later when the police tracked me down and the consequences of my last night on the drink played out through the court process, which was not an unusual situation for me. It had to be dealt with and the consequences followed me for many years. While I don't advertise my history, I don't hide from it either. It is part of who I am.

Looking back, I think I knew AA worked from my first exposure, but I didn't want to stop drinking. In my observation over the years if you don't want to stop drinking you won't. This was me; I didn't think my drinking was bad enough at the time to need AA. I thought "If I ever really need AA in the future I could come back when I'm old". I was lucky that I got back before my alcoholism killed me, or someone else.

In my professional capacity I have seen life-changing events fueled by alcohol destroy, or irreversibly change, plenty of lives. While I'm glad I avoided this when I was drinking, it was only by sheer luck, AA saved my life, gave me a life, and was my only chance. I've been sober for thirty-two years. The 6th of February 1990 was my last drink, but I have no doubt I'm a day-to-day proposition and just for today I don't drink. When tomorrow arrives, if it does, it will be today, and 'I don't drink today'.

> **Mike K** is 58 years of age, married with three adult children, none of which have ever seen him drink. He works as a lawyer, predominantly practising in the area of criminal law.

24

Davo

My first drink was on a school excursion at the age of fifteen. In Queensland the drinking age was twenty-one, in NSW it was eighteen. We went from Brisbane down to the Gold Coast and got on the piss. When I got home my mum said, "What's the matter with you?" I answered, "I got a touch of the sun" and mum said, "You better stay away from that sun, son."

I came from a non-drinking family. My mum hated alcohol because her dad was an alcoholic.

Because I lived at home it was hard to drink but as soon as I joined the Queensland police force it was 'pull your ears back' and from the age of seventeen I was in full flight from day one. Getting into heaps of trouble, a lot of car accidents and many fights. That was the normal shit that happened when I was pissed.

I was a daily drinker from seventeen to twenty-seven. I drove a car into a car showroom in Spring Hill in Brisbane. I'd been on the booze at work, and I met some 'sheila' later that night at a club and on the way back to her place I turned around the corner and went right through the showroom. Wrote the car off and got a bill for seventy grand. I didn't get done for drink driving. They took me to hospital, but I bolted.

I was sent as a constable to the Queensland country town of Miles. My drinking escalated and I was banned from two of the three pubs in Miles. My landlady there said "Oh, Mister Isherwood, you're a nice man, but when you drink you're terrible!"

A lot of the past I can't recall. But when I was drinking alcoholically, I do remember chasing a bloke across the Storey Bridge in Brisbane. When I called out "Stop! Stop!" he turned around and said, "Why don't you stop, no-one's chasing you!" I laughed and gave up the chase.

I first went to AA in 1983 and attended AA in Brisbane for a few months. I was sent by my employer who said I had to do something about my drinking. I thought it was unfair that I was being singled out. My work had a program for problem drinkers which was AA based and as a result I went to my first meeting on their say so. I had no intention of stopping.

The bloke who took me, Greg, was both my boss in the police force and my AA Sponsor. This might seem an unusual situation, but he was very persistent and kept taking me to the meetings. Once he went on holidays and I stopped going. I couldn't be bothered and had no intention of quitting drinking. It was only because my employer had intervened and said I could lose my job if I didn't stop drinking that I went to AA at all.

When I was a reluctant debutante in AA, and went weekly to a meeting at Kangaroo Point, I thought about two long-time members there, "If ever I get as mad as Ross Fitzgerald and Bob Noud, I'll give up the booze!" As it turned out that they were the two AA members who eventually helped me the most.

I was sent on a job to go to Tewantin to pick up a bloke who had committed numerous crimes. A partner and I left Brisbane at 2:00 pm. Our shift was from 2:00 pm to 10:00 pm. It normally took a couple hours to drive there. We got as far as the Kedron Park Hotel and my sidekick said, "I might get a six pack of beer for the trip" and I said, "You'd better get a dozen." We polished them off and we had a pub-a-thon all the way up. We called in at my uncle's house and drank everything he had, including the cooking wine.

When we called into Surf Air to try and get take-a-way, they were closed. But someone sold us a carton of beer at bar prices. Imagine how much a carton cost in those days! We arrived at Tewantin at midnight. The coppers there were most unhappy as they were waiting for us. After we picked the passenger up, we were supposed to drive the stolen car back. But we couldn't because we were too pissed. Yet we drove the police car sucking grog all the way back with the bloke in the back seat, who was terrified by our antics and wild driving.

When we got back to Brisbane, I tried to type up the paperwork which was all over the place and the CIB wouldn't accept him as a prisoner. So I got the shits and let him go and made arrangements for him to come in the next morning. Which he didn't!

At 3:00 am I promptly went to drink and carouse the nightclubs in Fortitude Valley, which was Brisbane's version of Kings Cross.

I stumbled home at about 7:00 am. As I arrived my immediate superior rang because the Police Commissioner had been rung at home. It seems I had abused someone at work about 2:00 am and they had made a complaint.

My wife answered and I called out "Tell him I'm sick" and my boss said, "Tell him he *will* be sick if he's not here by 8:00 o'clock!"

I fronted up to work pissed as a newt and was given a dressing down. As a proviso I was told I had to sort out the job because there were stolen goods all over the place and I had to front the Commissioner. The Commissioner was Terry Lewis who gave me one last chance. He told me that the next time I got drunk I'd be gone, and I believed him.

So, I went back to AA with a different attitude.

I've been sober for thirty-eight years now and attend meetings regularly. It was well known at work that I had given up the piss. About a year or so after I came back to the fellowship, Greg my sponsor drank again and another member, the late Bob Noud rang and told me. I decided to visit him, and Bob came with me.

On the piss, Greg was a changed man. Prior to drinking he was very well-presented and a thoughtful and rather spiritual person. But when we got to his home, he was an absolute mess. Watching the cricket and sucking on booze, he offered us a coffee and as we tried to hold a conversation, the camera panned across the cricket crowd and focused on a young woman with huge breasts and very short shorts. Greg leapt forward and yelled "Look at the knockers on her!" I was shocked! I had never seen him like that. Back on the booze he had a complete personality change.

After I was sober a long, long time, a prisoner who had escaped a minimum-security prison in Melbourne gave himself up in Toowoomba. The escapee broke down and sobbed and said, "I'm an alcoholic." To which a young constable said, "It's your lucky day! Our boss is the head of AA in Toowoomba!." Well, there are no heads or bosses in AA, but I'm certainly a very grateful and fortunate member.

> Now retired and an avid gardener, **Davo** was a long-serving member of the Queensland police force. Although he lives in Toowoomba, every Saturday he drives to South Brisbane to attend the 8:00 pm AA meeting at South Brisbane, which was founded in 1983 by Ross Fitzgerald.

25

Dick Love

The last six months of my drinking had seen great acceleration. I was a special education teacher and lived in Penrith. We had our first child. He's now almost fifty-four. He was nine months old when I came to my first meeting.

I was fortunate to meet Marion, my wife, about three years after arriving in Australia, so that would have been five years before coming to AA and with her help she got me clothing, she encouraged me. I wasn't stupid. There was an adult teacher training program when I was twenty-four and it was held as an annex of Sydney Teachers College and there were seventy of us who went through that course. There were about fifty Ugandan older ladies who were out here on a cultural exchange and we had an inspector of schools, who sort of guided the program. I excelled which is interesting because I didn't excel in my leaving certificate, the equivalent of the HSC in Ireland, mainly because I didn't want to.

I was interested in sport and nothing else. I was also probably unsettled and a bit of a dreamer, all of that. So anyway, I met Marion and she went to work while I went to Teacher's College and I subsequently was posted out where the University of Western Sydney is now, halfway between Pennington St Mary's at Werrington.

We had four hundred acres where the university is now. We had a school on the property and there were four houses with thirty boys in each house. Many of the children were of the First Nation stolen generation, but I had a rapport with them. I was the choirmaster and sports-master. I loved my job.

But the problem was I couldn't get home from school. I'd go for a drink at half past three and eventually, the other teachers, there were about fifteen of them, would come and conspire with Marion. The plan was that they would come with me to the Hotel in St Mary's, the Rex or the Wagon Wheel or to the Band Club. Eventually the Penrith leagues became the mecca and they would come with me at half past three and at five, one of them would stupidly suggest that I go home to my wife. By that stage I'd have had three or four schooners and being an alcoholic I wasn't going anywhere. I would eventually get home at all hours and Marion would be distressed and I was destroying any money that we had. I was a poker machine addict, I've had a lot of trouble with that over the years. I haven't played them for some time now and I hope I don't again. So that was the scenario, things weren't good at home. There were mixed circumstances leading up to me going to my first meeting. There were about four or five incidents over a period of months that I see now were accelerating my entry into AA.

I had a previous period when I was just over twenty-one and lived around the lanes of Surrey Hills, Redfern and Newtown. I played very good rugby for Randwick when I was twenty, and it took me not longer than twelve months to be evicted out of a flat that Randwick Reunion had given me. I had a cheque book but I didn't have any money in the bank so I used to write dodgy cheques. They would call me and were very kind to me and say "Could you put some money in the bank?"

In Ireland Jim and I were schoolmates and great friends and he followed me out here to Australia and ended up in Victoria. The lovely guy was not an alcoholic, just liked a few drinks. He was to be married to a girl from Bendigo, in Bendigo. Marion, pregnant with our first child. I went down to Melbourne on the Spirit of Progress. Jim met me and we drove to Bendigo on Friday, the day before the wedding, and out to a little country pub. We're drinking these thimbles. I thought they were probably either five or seven ounce glasses, but I was a schooner drinker and making fun of these pathetic small glasses. I have to report that if you drink thirty or forty it has the same effect. So I ended up in the back of a utility later that night, supposed to be there for the wedding. I had a new suit Marion had got for me. The wedding reception was on a rural property belonging to a Commonwealth Games cyclist.

The day after the wedding I was so drunk I fell into the edge of the fire and singed my suit. The next day I went back to Sydney on the Spirit of Progress. That broke down at about 5.00 am. This was May and I came into AA in June. It broke down outside Goulburn and I was freezing and had the shakes. I looked like an absolute derelict. Marion and her mother met me at Central Station and they were shocked by my appearance. Marion's mother was the most wonderful mother-in-law. She helped to disguise my alcoholism for other members of the family. She would help Marion buy Christmas and birthday presents saying they were from me. One Christmas I got a medical benefits cheque for our first son Sean and a rebate from Medibank that I put through the poker machine while Marion was in hospital, chronic stuff.

There was a memorable event that led to me going to my first meeting. I talked with a Canadian guy who shared a flat with an American guy who'd served in Vietnam. He was the first professional basketballer in Australia. They had just been accepted into rugby league. It was going to be the first rugby league game between Penrith and Cronulla. The game was on at 3:00 pm Saturday so I arranged to meet these two guys at 10:00 am. I hadn't met the American yet. There was an English marine I knew slightly who lived around the cul-de-sac. Anyway, I introduced him to the American marine who was a basketball player, about six foot ten and they were great mates, for two or three hours.

When I was in trouble I used to invite people home, so I invited the two marines and the Canadian home. I'm paralytic and Marion's in the bedroom and the next moment the marines decide they'll have a skirmish to decide who's the best marine. Marion is witness to all of this. It was chaotic. Now, that was a month before the final event.

I went to the leagues club after work and stayed until 1:30 am. I always got a lift home and that night it was with an army sergeant and his blonde wife. They came inside and Marion started querying this. When they eventually went home, in my drunken state I decided that the blonde wife better come back. I later started throttling Marion on the front lawn in a blackout, that was the worst thing that I've done. Marion recalls that later on that evening, I said "I need help." The next morning I woke up in a terrible state with the shakes, and I went up to the school with the shakes and I couldn't write on the blackboard. I'd had the shakes for months and couldn't write on the blackboard.

Marion went to a red telephone box, corner of 2nd Ave, Kingswood. She rang 000 and whoever was in the PMG department realised that Marion was in distress. She was a very empathetic woman and said to Marion, "Come back to this telephone box in one hour and I'll get somebody to help you." And she did. An hour later, she spoke to a man named Gordon at the public telephone box. He was the black sheep of a family from Wauchope that owned a tourist resort, 'Timber Town'. They owned all the timber up in the tablelands, a very wealthy family. He was a 'bender drinker' and never got permanently sober, but he opened AA meetings in Wentworth Falls, Kanwal on the coast, and Port Macquarie. He was the youngest country member of AA in 1949 in Australia. And you can read about him in a book called 'History of AA on the North Coast of NSW'.

Remarkably, what happened is that he came to Mosman and met Charles from Rosebay in the fifties and he was given a 'Big Book'. He took it back to Wauchope and lent the 'Big Book' to six chronic 'alkies' including two methylated spirit drinkers from the forestry camp, two publicans, Snowy Mac from Telegraph Point, and Ferris from Port Macquarie Hotel. So over a period of time he lent the Big Book to six chronic 'alkies' and not one of those six had another drink in their lives after reading that 'Big Book'. But Gordon lapsed every eight months or so. A wonderful man but he couldn't get sober for long, I think two years was the most time he actually got up.

So, he put Marion and I in the car that night, 21st of June 1968. And we had another man in the car called Tow Truck Barry, he died a few years ago. A rebellious character, a loveable rogue. I believe we had a lady in the car called Breathless Beryl, who suffered from emphysema and we went to Ryde and we met Mudgee Jack, Broken Hill Jack, Olga, and Herb from Hunters Hill. That was a big trip. My first meeting. The next night we went to a meeting at Narrabeen, even further. That began the journey, one day at a time, and that was over fifty-four years ago. I became a member of the Penrith group. We had a wonderful group there and later on I was a member at Woolloomooloo.

I first met Redfern Ross when we played cricket with the University of New South Wales and I was the captain of Penrith, one of the lower grades. We played at a place called Cook Park in St Mary's which was very unsophisticated. When visitors came from places like Mosman or NSW University we had to ask neighbours to boil the urn and we would congregate in a tent or go to the Wagon Wheels, that same pub, and Ross would complain there were no facilities for non drinkers. Anyway, we met that day and have been lifelong friends since.

> **Dick** is 54 years sober, retired, and a member of the Saratoga AA group. He volunteers for The Glen, a rehab for Indigenous men, where he supports the remedial English program.

26

Dave B

I grew up in Springfield, known now as West Moonah in Hobart. It was named after the old orchard estate and was also known as 'little Warsaw'. It was full of Polish refugees, my father being one of them, and that's why this is relevant because in Polish culture drinking in the home was pretty much accepted. My father gave me my first drinks in the sixties. It was often McWilliams sherry which was pretty rough. The range of alcohol available then was limited. I don't remember much of it. I didn't start drinking alcoholically until I was thirty-four when I moved to Canberra as a career public servant. I was one of those people where the disease was a slow burner, then in Canberra it suddenly took off.

I know it's unusual for someone like me to drink unproblematically for years and years but I am an example of someone who can't remember their first drink but can remember exactly when I crossed the thin red line into alcoholism. Because I drank uneventfully for years, that got me thinking that I would one day return to social drinking. I needed to understand that wasn't correct. I would never be able to drink with safety or drink normally.

I did a Bachelor of Science with a double major in physics. When I finished my honours year I needed to do a Graduate Diploma in computing which wasn't available where I lived. I got a transfer with public service to a training position in Canberra and built a career there. I lasted ten years and towards the end of that period I went into three detoxes. The Langton clinic back when it was a Twelve Step detox, and then McKinnon and after that the third detox at Basement 82 at RPA hospital. I had a rough time there because I'm trained to give precise details. That set the tone of that detox basically and it went downhill from there. Of course, I didn't drink when I was in the detox.

When I got home I drank again and I rang my sister. I was supposed to have treatment with a psychiatrist under the supervision of the workplace occupational health and safety people but when I turned up they smelled alcohol on my breath and the psychiatrist terminated our session. My sister very strongly suggested that I contact him again and I went there and that's when I got the prescription for an antidepressant. It was just up the street in Surrey Hills, only a couple of blocks away from where I lived.

That's where that journey started and then two or three days later I was starting to get sane enough to go to a meeting at the Salvation Army through the Bridge program. I pretty much stopped drinking that day. I started going to meetings every day for the rest of the week. Then on the Friday, I went to the meeting at Surry Hills and although I'd been there before I clashed with some of the people and it was fairly obvious that I didn't react to that well. I had a hip flask of whisky and that was my last drink but I kept going to meetings.

I will go next for what happened. I was working in the public service and in March 1996 John Howard came into power. Our project was trying to work with Canberra from Sydney which was problematic in itself. It had been extended quite a lot by this stage. The new Government said no way. We kept going back and forth and we were offered redundancies and I just couldn't cope with that. I didn't have any resources left to cope with it and I completely fell apart. I got a chronic fatigue condition. I could barely function or barely operate and the drinking didn't help. When things compounded, the drinking made things a hundred times worse and I started to take sick leave every week, as a result of that I was sent to the commonwealth medical officer. I said I was going back one day and I didn't make it. There's no way I was going to make it. I was completely unfit for work and I didn't know where to go. My boss was supportive, luckily and sent me back to the medical officer and they said you're on leave until you get better or your leave runs out.

I was on this sort of arrangement when I first got well. They knew about the psychiatrist, and I was under his supervision and within two or three weeks I was told to start getting a job. But my job didn't exist because of what had happened with the change of Government. So I promptly applied for another one, and thanks to the Y2K bug, I got a job very easily. Sick as I was, I got a job in the state public service which gave me the security I needed.

I always struggled in Hobart to get a job but as soon as I left and went to Canberra and Sydney I never had much trouble. All this mixes in together, that's why I paint the whole picture and so my last two or three weeks of drinking were intermittent. I'd been drinking around the clock before I went to the detox. I had a week in detox, drank when I came home, drank for three or four days, then had three or four alcohol free days, then had one brief drink and I didn't touch it again. I haven't touched it since.

Because I drank safely for about twenty years, I needed to find out where the thin red line was which was utterly vital to understand. I had to find out it was irreversible because I assumed that I could drink safely because I'd done that for so many years. It was crucially important for me to understand I wouldn't be able to go back to normal social drinking.

I realised I understood nothing about spirituality at all. I'd been talking to psychics and astrologists, and my honours degree was in astronomy. The reason I say that is because you could not get two fields further apart than astrology and astronomy. They are diametrically opposite ends of the spectrum. For someone with my background to do that was unusual.

It was my path out of Springfield and the less salubrious parts of Hobart. That stuff was really important too. It was an orchard estate that transitioned into a suburb, but the land was sold in dribs and drabs and it took a long time to sell. The streets where we lived didn't have proper kerbs and gutters so it was really rough and took many years to improve. Springfield went through a gradual transition from a lot of migrants who had little education and mostly worked in factories, to a modest working class suburb.

My father came from a subsistence farm straight from 'Fiddler on the Roof', Eastern Poland. He came to Australia with nothing and virtually no english. My father and mother were from vastly different social backgrounds, in fact, it was an enormous chasm.

My father went through some horrendous experiences during World War 11. He left Poland literally at the point of a gun. His village is now part of Ukraine; it was moved further west in the Potsdam agreement in 1945. He was in the very south east and in a very difficult situation. He was traumatised. As a kid, the domestic situation set me up for being anxious.

I got to university and didn't like it so I went to the public service. I did my graduate diploma in computers and that was an absolute full time job and very hard work. Academically much easier than a science degree, and when I graduated I got married, which was a disaster for about seven years, and I drank pretty much socially then. When that broke up my drinking got worse but there's a combination of things at play here.

Over time, the pressure and politics of working in the public service for a few years and those circumstances triggered off my own trauma. It wasn't diagnosed until I changed sponsors when I was about ten years sober. I was talking to a Vietnam war veteran and he explained what it was, and then let me come to my own conclusion. It's not really until you can hear the words you can work it out. He was smart enough to let me work it out, as much as I understand. The suggestion was not to worry too much about trying to work out where it came from, concentrate on treating it and in time it has proved to be a very good idea.

> **Dave** has been secretary of a meeting in his local area several times.

27

Barry R

The morning after my father's funeral I awoke in my childhood bedroom; we had family and friends come back to the family home from the cemetery for a traditional gathering. Some of my friends had flown from interstate to give me support. At most funeral's, friends are there for the people who are left and as family disappeared and I was left with friends, I drank more. I wasn't plastered or anything but my best friend had suggested I slow down. The next day when they all left I woke up with the thought "Why am I doing this? This cannot continue." It was a time of reflection.

When I woke up that next day there wasn't a plan of action, there was no shortage of food in the house, there was cleaning up to be done. My mother needed to work things out, but dad had been in a nursing home and she had a good routine. So for me it was an awakening that I had to live my life for me. I had to be responsible as I had to care for mum. I had to worry about me, my then wife and our three kids. My mum was a strong and organised woman but still needed me around for a couple of days.

My parents were good people and didn't drink, and as their only living child they put all their efforts into giving me all the good things in life. I had an excellent education which pushed me to study and I performed well enough to get into Sydney Uni. I graduated with an honours degree, and a place in Melbourne Uni Master's program. I did my Masters over four years. I got a great job with a car and a housing loan, made great friends and travelled a lot. I loved living in Melbourne and the freedom of not living with my family.

Upon graduation I got married and shortly after joined an international company, got promoted to a newly established business in Brisbane. My wife returned to uni to undertake doctoral studies and our three children were at elite private schools. On the outside life looked good.

When I had my own business, I would reward myself after work with a couple of glasses of wine. My wife always thought I should come home and drink with her. Sometimes I would be finishing things off, doing filing, waiting for overseas phone calls so we had the office and car space in Queen Street. We lived in Red Hill so it wasn't a big drive home.

I was content, being in the office and getting things done. I wasn't in a great rush to get home. That's life and you have to be true to yourself. At that stage my eldest son had finished school and my second son was in year eleven and my daughter was just starting high school. The boys went to a leading Catholic School and the girl, to a Grammar School. My wife was doing postgraduate studies in law. We were very social. My view was to keep the marriage together until the kids finished school.

I had been thinking about stopping drinking but my wife didn't want to stop. A good excuse looking back. Easy for me. The idea of stopping came to me after the funeral. I was overweight, eating the wrong things and not doing any exercise. One of my school friends said, "Looks like the next funeral we will go to might be yours." He said that at the funeral. The guy is a lawyer and a medical doctor and what he said really threw me.

I had first gone to AA to keep my wife happy by attending the 'twelve seminar program' she had heard of. The day after the funeral I called Bob, a man I had met when I attended some AA meetings and he simply said, "Son, don't have a drink today and get yourself to a meeting."

After the funeral I returned to Brisbane, and went back to AA. My wife and I had a meeting with Bob because she wanted to keep drinking. This business of "You're going to a twelve seminar program" was for her because she wanted me to learn how to 'control my drinking' so I could drink with her at home. At first when I had gone to AA I wanted to learn how to control my drinking. Very quickly you learn in AA that if you want what it has to offer, you have to take it on its terms. My wife and I gave up alcohol a couple of weeks later and both lost 18 kilos.

I had separated from my wife and two of my children came with me to Indonesia and we started a new life, the first rule of which was 'dad does not drink.' We rebuilt our lives over four years before I was ready to commit to another relationship.

I grew up in a family that accepted you had to take 'life on life's terms'. My mother is a very firm believer in that and when I talked to her, she said "If that's what you have to do, that's what you have to do". My parents were not big drinkers. We always had alcohol in the house but my parents wouldn't drink for months.

Bob (later my sponsor) was wonderful from the very first phone call. He said very simple things. He said I was an immensely complicated person and the fact I was underlining the Big Book in week one meant I should keep it simple. He said "There is a tendency for people like you to make it a science. I think you need to listen to people and see the similarities." This taught me how important it is to listen to the similarities and ignore the differences, and of the importance of regular meetings. Listening to others who were lawyers, accountants and had a similar work profile to me helped me a great deal because I could identify with them.

I heard early on from Long John Silver who said "Folks, there's good news and there's bad news. The good news is you can leave this meeting and need never drink again one day at a time. The bad news is if you're an alcoholic person you're going to spend the rest of your life with alcoholics. It's up to you to decide whether they are sober ones or pissed ones."

This was critical information. I still spent a lot of time with school friends who drank but I've had to learn not to drink with them and to escape if I had to. In reality I had to change a lot of my school, uni and professional friends especially when they would say "We don't trust someone who won't drink with us." My second wife has a medical issue and cannot drink and her family don't drink either. My two brothers-in-law don't drink.

During the six months before my father's death I was doing the 'twelve seminar program' and the message permeated but I didn't really take it on board. One day it dawned on me that drinking wasn't for me, I didn't want to feel horrible. I didn't drink a lot in one sitting but I'd drink for a long time, and the accumulative effect was that at the end of the day I was dried out. I thought "There's got to be a better life."

That was the seminal moment and it had been coming for a long time. I was trying to lose weight and eat properly and exercise and do things. Alcohol was full of calories and I felt dreadful, I was over eating and drinking into the night and eating lots of junk food, and I thought the answer had to be elsewhere. I was trying to delay the effects of alcohol, and I thought my whole life was driven by this. I had to stop this driving my life. That was the realisation. I needed to be a normal person and be healthy. If I had gone on that way I was going to die.

Today I am fitter, I exercise regularly and my circulation is much better. I get the natural hormones from exercise which make me feel good to be alive. The action moment was waking up after my father's funeral and thinking "I don't want to be like this."

My period in the wilderness was important. I kept working and accepted an overseas assignment for twelve months. Frankly, I just worked, ate healthy meals and exercised. I kept going to meetings and found Saturday night meetings filled an important void in my life. I always thought "If I'm in a meeting from 8 - 9:30 pm on a Saturday night I won't drink." It worked for me. I did find a home group and learned the lingo. I listened and learned how different people can enrich my new story. I have learned to choose friends who don't drink. If we have people come to our home now we send the half-bottles home with them. They don't say no.

Not drinking in business rarely causes an issue as long as you pay at least your share of the bill. I had to learn many things and my classroom was AA and talking to people I got to see regularly and asking my sponsor lots of real life questions.

> **Barry** has been sober twelve years, one day at a time, works in the financial industry and has three children.

28

Liz Joy

I was a binge drinker and drinking on weekends. I hadn't gone back to drinking every day as I had before, and had only been drinking with my friends and neighbours when we met on the weekends. My last drink was half a glass of red wine, and because it didn't taste very nice I took a few sips and poured it out, I really didn't want any more. I had been to the doctor because I was so upset and I'd started taking antidepressants. My marriage was in trouble. That might have had some effect on the taste of it, it was vinegary. For me it was hard to get alcohol in my life at the time as I was controlled by my husband. I had to drink wine because he did, but I preferred to drink whiskey. So I drank 'vinegar' as I called it because I wanted to get drunk and because I wanted to get out of it. That was really my last drink.

Before my last drink, when we separated, I started drinking every day to dull the pain but it wasn't working any more. In my head I thought this isn't good for me and I will stop, but I quickly reverted to weekend binge drinking. That was my default position, drinking with neighbours on the weekend. One Thursday night I went to marriage counselling with my husband and I thought it went well, but on the Friday when I saw my husband he told me he wanted a divorce. That was a week before I got to AA.

Nothing in my life was going to plan and everything I had believed in had changed completely. It was like I was a speck of dirt and there was a whole mountain in front of me, it was David and Goliath and I was smaller than David. The whole family unit was dysfunctional and had been for a long time. My children were abusing me. My son was self isolating and gaming, my daughter was swearing and yelling and screaming at me constantly. My husband was away or with girl friends and I was alone in my mind. Everyone was around me but I was so alone. I was alone in my own family. People who were supposed to love me didn't. I had a vision that the only thing that would help me was to stop drinking. It was the gateway to my life as it is now and the only hope I had. I had nothing in my life at all. It was either stop drinking or 'go out of the world' and I was too chicken to 'go out of the world' and I still am.

A month before I separated from my husband I had researched Alcoholics Anonymous, and as I was coming away from that confrontation with him the AA meeting was starting as I walked past. I knew there was an AA meeting there and I was in tears and didn't know what to do. I ended up going to the meeting that night, and the next Thursday I came back because everyone told me to. I stopped drinking on 19th July 2015.

I don't remember the meeting too much but I do remember the warmth that was shown to me. I don't remember clearly what I said but I copied what everyone else was saying because I didn't want to be different and said I was alcoholic. All I knew is that this was the place that could help me stop drinking.

I was trying to hold back the tears because of the divorce and I was thinking "What's going to happen?" My whole life had collapsed in front of me. At that stage the only decision I could control was me not drinking, I had no control over anything else. It was one foot in front of the other. The meeting gave me hope. There was hope and a feeling that I wasn't alone. There was something in that meeting that engulfed me and hugged me, and I'm not a huggy person. I must have really needed it. I was crying for the whole meeting.

Before I came to the meetings all of my friends were my husband's friends so when we divorced I lost my friends, except for a few neighbours. I was initially too frightened to go on Facebook because I thought I might have my identity stolen, but on Facebook I found old friends I lost because of my marriage. I should never have married that guy because he was so different to me. The only thing we had in common was alcohol and it was bound to fail and probably should have finished before it did. I stayed in that marriage because of my religious beliefs.

I was adopted and grew up wondering if I was going to be sent back. I used to overthink everything, watch people very closely, and found it hard to trust anyone. I started drinking at fourteen. I grew up in a religious baptist family who didn't drink alcohol, although my dad's brother was alcoholic, but we didn't have much to do with him. I was a good girl and law abiding. I went to a church-based club and was taught that drugs and alcohol were so bad and I promised not to drink. In my mind I said it was too bad for us and I would never drink but when I had that first drink it was 'wow' and it made me so happy, so happy. I had three drinks and it really affected me. It was scotch and dry and it was great. We were at a friend's party and because of the ginger ale mum and dad didn't know I was drinking alcohol. I was a teenager and was just trying to survive with the hormones and social stuff and drinking alcohol was really good. The only reason to drink was to get drunk.

I was well into my adult years before I thought I might have a problem. Waking up every weekend not fully functional, sleeping in every weekend, out late, and that's when it dawned on me. When I spoke to my husband he said we were 'functional alcoholics' and we just laughed it off. We were financially ok then and everything was going right for us. I realise now it starts off like a tornado and it's a big cloud up the top and it funnels down and it leaves destruction. That was my soul and I had nothing left.

The AA meetings were the only thing that gave me a sense of calmness. I would go once a week at first then I started going more, Wednesday, Friday and Saturday. At first my head was so foggy I couldn't read anything and I couldn't understand much and it took a long time for my mind to come back to me. I couldn't listen much at all. I thought it was the trauma of the separation, but the Gumdale meeting on Wednesday gave me relief. The women's meeting on a Monday also helped a great deal and there were a lot of younger women, thirty to forty year olds, who I could identify with. I just knew there was love in there.

It took years to really know what was going on in my life. I didn't believe I was alcoholic for a long time, then it dawned on me, it was my thinking. It's alcoholic thinking. It's how I think that matters, that's what made me believe I'm alcoholic. Not how much I drank or if I drank in the park or at a posh dinner. So I'm seven years into this journey and I've just heard that 'feelings aren't facts'. Normally I think my feelings are my facts! I understand what they mean by this is it doesn't matter how I feel, the fact is that every day I'm not drinking I'm doing ok.

I love the meetings. I trust a few people now and I love to see them and consider them my friends. I've been sober for seven years and still think I'm a baby in AA. The meetings give me hope but I'm still very much a pup.

> Liz lives in Brisbane and is secretary for a Friday night meeting. She is a hairdresser, community volunteer and avid gardener.

29

Ukrainian George

I was not in a good place either physically or in my head. I had worked my way down in the qualities of jobs that I had and quality of people that I knew. I didn't know anybody who didn't drink or do drugs or both and I didn't like the people I knew. I didn't know what to do and I was working as a delivery boy for an independent pizza place. I was drinking everyday and always had a cask of wine in the fridge. I wasn't eating very well. The pizza place kept me fed and I was stealing from him. I was getting my dealer to ring up and order ridiculous numbers of pizzas and not collect them. At the end of the night my boss would give them to me rather than throw them out and I would take them to my drug dealer's place on the way home.

I was sick and tired of being sick and tired and just didn't know what to do next. I'd done everything, I'd had my fifteen minutes of fame, I had left a mark in film, theatre and television. I wasn't stupid but I had no idea that it was the alcohol and drugs that had put me in this position. I was living under someone's house in an illegal flat, the ceiling was well less than six feet high and I shared that space with five cats and a dog and many cockroaches and spiders and luckily the dog liked eating spiders. I'd come home and turn on the light and the dog would go berserk running into nooks and crannies biting spiders.

I came home and didn't know what to do, I just screamed out "I can't do this anymore, I don't know what to do." I know I screamed it out because my landlord called out and asked me if I was alright. I felt embarrassed and the next day I came to and without any thought or pre planning or anything, I went into action. I knew a doctor who used to prescribe methadone to me. I was in Newmarket and he was in Buranda and I bussed it over to his clinic and just walked past the receptionist into his office and he got really shocked. He spurted out to me "I'm not giving you any methadone." I said "I don't want methadone, I don't know what I want. I just can't do this any more."

And he looked at me and wrote a note, then another note, then put the first note in an envelope. On the second note he wrote Biala on the envelope and said "Take this to Biala." I said "I have no idea what you're talking about" and he said "If you're serious you'll find out." I didn't even know what he meant by the word serious.

Anyway, I asked the next bus driver "Do you know where Biala is?" He said "I go right past there" so I got on the bus to this place Biala. I didn't know what it was and I went in and the receptionist opened the envelopes. I just stood there and a door opened, I went in and they handed me a pair of hospital pyjamas and I thought "Oh no, not this again." I'd been through the ringer of detox and rehabs and didn't think I had a problem with alcohol and drugs. It was always about getting people off my case.

I drank and drugged my way through that detox. They sent me home after a week and asked me to ring everyday and not have a drink. I kept arguing with them that I didn't have a problem with alcohol. I couldn't see how stopping drinking could change my situation. I went back to that little flat under the house. I bought a car from my landlord. I was on Social Security. I rang Biala every day, I don't know why but I rang everyday at 1:00 pm or 2:00 pm and after a few days they said "You need to be here tomorrow by 3:00 pm."

I finished off the wine that I had left in the fridge and smoked a joint and got down there and they told me I was booked into rehab. I said "I don't know what the point of that is, I've done plenty of rehabs" and they said "Well you came in here to detox and now you're alcohol-free you can go to the rehab. I said to the counsellor "I went to a party last night" and she said "What! Just get on the bus and good luck!"

They had a lot of counsellors there and a lot of different recovery models, controlled drinking, harm minimisation, cognitive therapy, and a Twelve Step counsellor. I knew about AA as I used to pop my head into meetings from time to time and have a feed. There was always cake and coffee in the kitchen. I was told, "Help yourself to what's there." At one meeting I ate all the cake and at the end of the meeting they came looking for the cake and I was wiping crumbs off my mouth, it was someone's anniversary and I had eaten the whole thing. I had an inability to accept any sort of personal responsibility. I had to make it their fault that they didn't tell me not to eat the cake. I had many of those moments during the sixteen years when I first went to an AA meeting with a friend believing I was there for support. I could have stayed and gotten sober then, but I didn't.

In the rehab I got this Twelve Step counsellor and she asked what I'd been doing since I got out of detox and I told her. She said "Thank you for telling me, you shouldn't be here. Every day we'll do a urine test and make sure the levels are declining." "How much are you drinking?" I said, "Not much." "What, weekends, once a week?" I answered "No, everyday." "How long have you been doing that?" "Daily for about twenty-two years."

She asked, "Do you take any other drugs?" I said, "I smoke pot." "How much, weekly, once a week?" I replied, "Not much." "How long have you been doing that?" "Every day for about twenty-two years." She said "Do you take any other drugs?" I said, "No. I don't take pills but I use heroin whenever I can." "How long has that been going on?" I said, "About twenty years." She leaned forward and said "Do you understand that a drug is a drug? Alcohol is a drug. A drug is a drug is a drug. There are no hard drugs, there are no soft drugs, there are only drugs." For people like you there are just drugs.

She said "While you're here, try not to use any drugs, don't drink and don't use any other drugs while you're here. Do you think you can do that?" I was always told if you pick up a drink or a drug you would get kicked out but she didn't say that.

She offered me this thing as a suggestion and I said "I'll try" and she let me go. A week later she called me back, "All your tests show you haven't been drinking or using any form of mind altering substance. How do you feel?" I replied, "Have you noticed how blue the sky is?" A big thing! I'd lifted my head up the first time in I don't know how long.

She then said, "I'd like you to go Alcoholics Anonymous meetings while you're here." I told her "It's rubbish, it's for older people, not for people like me, I'm young, (I was twenty-eight), in my prime of life, it was a substitute addiction, it's a cult, it's money making, they take advantage of vulnerable people." I argued and she sat there and listened to my protests. Then said "If you don't go to AA you're going to have to leave." I sat back and did the maths in my head. I'm getting three meals a day, I'm not paying rent, I'm saving the dole to pay off my car, I don't have to do anything here. "I'll give it a go." I concocted a story in my mad mind. I wasn't stupid but I tried to rationalise everything within the madness in my head.

She said, "I will give you three days to think about it and then you either go to AA or pack up and leave." I couldn't accept anyone else's opinion without turning it around and making it mine. I had to be the winner, so I concocted this story that the rehab was getting money for everyone who went to AA and therefore by going to the meetings I would be helping them to stay in business. So after three days she asked "What are you thinking?" I told her "Yeah probably." I would humble myself before her explaining what a good job they were doing with real losers, not people like me but real down and outs but they could do with the funding so I would concede to go. Once again, I was told to "Just get on the bus," a real metaphor in my life which I had ignored three times before. Then I went to my first AA meeting sober.

I still didn't believe alcohol and drugs had anything to do with it but I found a group of people to be vulnerable with at those meetings that I had never experienced before. Today when I look at that I think it's because I was never available for anybody. I was always trying to work out what people wanted from me. It took me a long time to understand that putting a drink in me made a bad idea seem good and unacceptable behaviour acceptable. I was just an alcoholic. I thought I was controlling it but with each drink I was actually just feeding it. I was the last to know. Something I thought was a cult, I'm an old fellow now. I'm thirty-one years sober and comfortable in my own skin, so we shall see.

George has been sober thirty-one years and is secretary of the Thursday East Brisbane meeting. He lives in Brisbane, and has one adult son who has never seen him drink.

30

Kate G

My last geographical found me in Nicaragua. I'd tried to save myself so many times but couldn't so thought I'd head to Central America and save the rainforest and children instead. I would usually start each night alone at a local restaurant, have a meal and a few drinks to try to celebrate my existence and hopefully meet people later on. The drink gave me the ability to communicate and connect with other people.

Anyway this particular night was much like all the others, I had my meal and a few beers – and headed to a bar. I don't really remember going in but it was local, cosy and not far from the restaurant. I was in San Juan del Sur, a southern coastal town in Nicaragua. It appeared really inviting, as bars do, and the people looked to be having fun. I got chatting with them and started hanging out. I was going up to the bar and buying rum, and drinking with the group. I remember at some stage during the evening people were talking about what age people were and it came around to me. One of the guys said I think you are just over fifty. I was absolutely mortified. I couldn't believe it. People had always thought I was much younger than I was and I was still only forty-four! It was not that long ago, maybe six weeks prior, that I was in a place in Panama with some much younger women who were complimenting me on how youthful I looked and thought my age was around twenty-seven. Not bad, ageing about twenty-three years in six weeks! I was shocked to hear that all the people in the group agreed, plus or minus a year! My normal drinking pattern kicked in, getting faster and faster, and I'm definitely one of those drinkers that once I pick up, I can't stop.

Later in the evening I remember buying cheap local rum over the bar and also topping up my drink from one of the bottles of rum I had underneath the table. I was drinking so fast. Not sure how or why but I had a couple of bottles of rum in my bag. Maybe I bought them for security so as to not run out, maybe I bought them for later on, maybe I was planning on drinking alone. I was found out and told not to do that and what bad form that was. A bottle of rum only cost about $5 and a drink over the bar was probably only 50c. I was embarrassed I was doing it because it was so cheap. I probably continued, I can't remember, as I had no power over this. By this stage I'd run out of money and went back to my hostel which wasn't far away. I never knew how I did it, however, I managed to crawl my way back to my hostel room, no matter where I was on my geographicals, and went upstairs to get the money. I had left my bag in the bar and when I came back to pay, my bag was outside on the street and the bar doors were locked. My 'new friends' were still inside now sitting around the bar with the lights gently dimmed. The owner refused to let me in and didn't even want my money. This absolutely killed me, I was devastated, bewildered and felt despair, to be refused and not let back into the comfort, and companionship of others in the bar. I picked up my bag, fell over in an alleyway and smashed the remaining bottle of rum.

I don't remember the rest of the night. I definitely remember waking the next day having that familiar awful sinking dread that I had woken up with for so, so many years. The shame, guilt, remorse, loneliness. I guess that you get these feelings as a result of repeating the same things over and over again, always expecting a different result. I'd promised myself that I would only go out for one or two and stop like everyone else did, or at least be able to keep things under control. As I walked out onto the verandah, I remember looking up to the sky and it was going red, and it was the middle of the day. I had a very strong feeling that I was going insane again, that I was quickly losing the fickle bits of sanity I was dearly holding on to. An impending doom, terror set in. I'd been there before, however, there was something a little bit different this time. I'd been on antidepressants and medication for anxiety for years and had been prescribed medication to sleep and reduce my substance use. At times I had locked myself in the house where I couldn't look out the windows, unemployable and on benefits, couldn't face any reality, wouldn't eat, hell on Earth as it was. I definitely didn't want to go back there as I was afraid I would end up even worse. I felt like there was this little space, a moment of grace, I actually asked for a little help not to go insane again.

Returning to sit on the bed of the hostel I thought my best solution was to leave everything at the hostel, go out to the jungle and just surrender myself. I thought that was the only thing I could offer the entire world. I honestly felt that I was just wasting oxygen at that time, and to die out there in the jungle was my only choice. I gave myself about a week to live. That was the way that I felt despite just spending months doing volunteer work in Panama.

At this time something else came into my mind which I've never thought of before, and that was maybe I could ask for help with my addiction problem. I logged onto my small laptop and searched for 'help', 'addiction' and 'Nicaragua'. I was fortunate that I had been learning Spanish while volunteering, as a little man popped up on Skype and suggested that I come down to this place for the weekend near the capital and see what they could do to help me. I had an alternative to the jungle. I thought I could try out this place for a couple of days and happily get back on my way and continue my travels through Central, and maybe South America.

At this time I also had a massive abscess on my breast that I was having to tend to, as when I was in Costa Rica traveling between Panama and Nicaragua, I must have got bitten and I didn't get it seen to. I ended up in a small town in Costa Rica for about four weeks to have it diagnosed and drained twice daily and get daily antibiotic injections. At this hostel I had already had 'my really last big drink', I swore off drinking. During this one, I ended up miles away from the town I was staying in, in a little roadside bar in the middle of nowhere with only people speaking Spanish. Some local asked me if I wanted to go out to his ranch with him in his pick-up truck. I was very drunk and jumped in. By this stage I had no money, no shoes, no issues! He appeared to have no ulterior motive and I remember him asking me over and over, "Are you okay with this?" and 'You don't have to do this." He knew my state and maybe was actually looking out for me – as had happened many times before, and am grateful for the times that I wasn't taken advantage of. Anyway I said "I'm happy, let's go."

I don't know how long we were driving down the road, however, quite a while, I decided to get out. I asked him to stop and I just jumped out of the truck. I didn't have a clue where I was, which way the town was that I was staying in, just fields on each side of the road. It was the middle of the night, dark with faded moonlight as it was raining. I walked past a cemetery in a field. It was an eerie experience. I was so angry, so angry with myself that I had done it again. I was screaming, crying, yelling to the heavens as I had promised myself I wasn't going to put myself in this situation again. End up with no money, no dignity, no shoes, absolutely nothing, and that I couldn't connect my brain with my mouth. My thinking was very lucid. I had drunk myself sober, the alcohol had stopped working. I had been on a bender drinking for days, well actually months, years, thirty years. But anyway I remember being so angry at myself declaring again that I would never ever get drunk like that again. I finally made it back to the hostel after the sun had risen, guzzled some benzos, which were a constant in my daily routine, and woke from my final party trick - wetting the bed.

I was working seriously on rebuilding trust in myself as I had lost it all after continuing to do things that I swore I would never do again. I held fast and remained alcohol free for the next couple of weeks under my doctor's orders and my own desperation to allow my injury to heal. After about three weeks I brushed myself off and got my backpack in order to head north to Nicaragua. Upon leaving the hostel, the owner handed me a copy of 'Rachel's Holiday' by Marian Keyes stating that I probably won't like it, as he had only seen me mainly 'dry' with a tropical injury. Little did he know how instrumental that book would be in changing my life.

Fast forward to the hostel in Nicaragua, I was still trying to tend to my wound in a dazed and confused state. I was hopeless at looking after myself and was so frustrated that I had to follow this methodical procedure so I didn't end up dying from a tropical disease in some long-protracted manner. I wasn't afraid of dying, in fact I had tried very hard a number of times to die both quickly and slowly. I did an online quiz to test whether I was an alcoholic. I only ticked eighteen of the twenty boxes, so I didn't think 100% that alcohol was the problem, it was the fact I couldn't just have one that was the problem. That and the fact that life wasn't as I wanted it to be. I was reading 'Rachel's Holiday' which I now understand was assisting me gain identification of alcoholism, addiction, and behaviours. I was sick and tired of being sick and tired. I was absolutely exhausted.

A couple of days later I decided I might try and find this man where I could stay for a couple of days and get some proper respite. I packed up my stuff and headed to the bus station. I was told it would take about three or four buses over eight hours. I got on the last bus and let them know where I wanted to go. It was on-route however not at a stop, I remember them stopping, throwing out my back-pack and pushing me out of the bus. I thought "I'm a white western girl. What's that about?" The fact that I must have looked shocking, stunk, and asked to be dropped off at 'Centro de Addictions', would have a lot to do with it! I crawled my way to the entry gates. There was a security guard with a big machine gun protecting the imposing buildings surrounded by high white enclosed barbed wire walls and fences. I said I needed some rest and I'd come to see Jose. He let me in and the people took me downstairs and I was seen by the doctor and nurses. I felt like this was home and these people would be able to take care of me.

After a couple of days I was able to meet the Director, Jose. I shared briefly what was going on with me. He disclosed that he was an alcoholic and addict and had been in recovery for years. It was the first time that I had ever knowingly met and spoken with a recovering alcoholic or addict. I didn't know that such a concept existed and that this was even possible. He knew that I needed to (and would) stay longer than the weekend, however, kept it simple and in the day. He didn't want to scare me off before I had even been introduced to the concept of recovery. I asked him "Why now? Why have I finally come into recovery, when I still had a few bucks in my back-pocket and half of my health?" I certainly had had my fair share of rock bottoms involving hospitals, institutions, money issues, relationship breakdowns all as a direct result of substance abuse. He kindly shared that I had a spiritual rock-bottom, I had finally run out of all ideas and was unable to continue running on self-will.

I'd been to that many councillors, psychiatrists, doctors who had prescribed so much medication. I've swapped drugs, countries, relationships, everything I could throughout thirty years of active addiction. It was the first time that I had come across an alcoholic in recovery who could actually understand what I was going through. I was introduced to the Twelve Steps on the first day of the treatment program. I identified immediately with the first step, 'We are powerless over alcohol and our lives had become unmanageable.' I was obviously powerless as I had attempted and failed to stop and stay stopped daily for thirty years, my life was certainly unmanageable – I had just arrived in a treatment centre on the other side of the world with a backpack full of benzos.

I understand now that I was just an untreated garden variety alcoholic/addict, who had a Higher Power waiting for me to be ready. I was provided with the gift of desperation, and that actively working a Twelve Step program is the only solution for me.

Ironically despite all I went through that last night in San Juan del Sur, it was not my last drink. It was the following evening when I found another restaurant to eat in, again alone. I was drinking juice and the lovely owner offered me some of her moonshine. I said "No," she asked again, really wanting me to try her home made drink, while I was sitting there all alone. I was defenceless against the first drink.

I left the treatment centre in Nicaragua and went into a rehabilitation program in Dublin, Ireland for the following seven months to continue her journey in recovery. Now coming up to nine years clean and sober, one day at a time, I'm back in Australia and have built a solid career using my science background.

Kate still has a passion for travel, however, now heads to a meeting when she arrives. Being a sober alcoholic is so much more fun.

31

Kaz K

I can't remember much of the last twenty-four hours of my drinking. Drinking started very early for me and by the time I was fourteen I was drinking so much I was kicked out of the local roller-skating club. So that gives you an indication of where I was headed. Interestingly though I managed to qualify in a profession and for the most part appeared to be living a 'normal' life while drinking and taking all sorts of drugs on a daily basis. Not everyone was fooled though and some tried to intervene but I wasn't having any of that and went to great lengths to avoid anyone who was 'on to me'.

Towards the end of my drinking I spent time in South East Asia, India and Nepal with my best friend and drinking buddy, Neal. It was becoming really hard to function; to work, pay the bills, and support what had become an expensive habit - drinking and using drugs. I thought it would be a smart move to travel around Asia where alcohol and drugs were cheaper and stronger. As a result, my already failing health progressed rapidly. After some months we came back to the Gold Coast. I was unemployable and very unwell.

The last twenty-four hours of my drinking started about a week before. It began with the visit of Neal's friend, Sharyn, who was a cocktail waitress in Hobart. She was out dancing, pissed of course, and fell over and broke her arm and couldn't work, so there was an invitation to "Come on up to the Gold Coast Darling! It's Fabulous!" Sharyn arrived with wine in her suitcase and whingeing about her brother drinking all her wine. I thought "'God she's a mess, she must be an alcoholic."

Years before I was working in a psychiatric hospital and used to take the alcoholic patients to AA meetings, so I knew about Alcoholics Anonymous. At the time I would listen to their stories and think "God I drank more than that last night. What a pack of losers." Little did I know ... in fact in retrospect I knew nothing really about alcoholism or AA. I was a registered nurse and doing psychiatric nurse training and drinking and taking drugs every day. The Director of Nursing was onto me though and told me I was a 'sickly' type of person, which was true, there were not many weeks when I wasn't off sick. I once took six weeks annual leave and went to Indonesia and was using a lot of heroin so decided to stay longer without letting anyone know. When I returned my car was about to be repossessed, the rent on my house was way overdue, my job was tenuous, and my family was about to notify the Australian Embassy.

Back to the week before the last drink, Sharyn spent a lot of time crying and was obviously down and depressed, and then she attempted suicide. This led to a discussion around her having a drinking problem and a suggestion that a meeting of AA would be the solution. She agreed with that idea. The main thing on my mind was that I didn't want to deal with a dead body and police coming to the house. When I was nineteen years old, a very good friend died of an overdose of alcohol and heroin, sadly the first of many, and I didn't want to go through that again.

Now, Sharyn was a cocktail waitress, so I thought it would be a shame to let her skills go to waste. I thought that if she went to AA she would stop drinking and suggested that we have a party before we went to the meeting. I called this 'The Party to End All Parties'. We ordered in a selection of spirits and whatever else we needed for the cocktails and any drugs we could get our hands on; it was going to be a fabulous party.

By this stage in my drinking, I wasn't partying very much. Along with alcohol my drugs of choice were downers; heroin, sedatives and hypnotics, benzos and barbs, and I took far too many for far too long. All we could get hold of quickly was speed and cocaine, oh well, I didn't care really, I'd take anything. The party started mid-afternoon for us because of course we had to try all the cocktails! I think I went into a blackout before people arrived and have patchy memories of what happened that night. I remember at some point shooting up speed in the bedroom with Neal and him asking, "Can you take my pulse?" It was 240 beats a minute and he said, "Great I can go again," and of course we did. The idea of risk management never existed, there were no limits, I always wanted more. I used to carry a copy of the MIMS (a comprehensive drug reference) and there were many well-worn pages. I took pride in my knowledge of all things drug related.

The night was a bit of a blur, but I have vague memories of biting Neal and him trying to push me over the balcony or down the steps, or both. I think a group of people crashed the party and caused some damage. It was one of those familiar, chaotic, parties that I knew well from my earlier drinking days. It was awful really and I remember feeling withdrawn, fragile and frayed, and feeling like shit the next day.

I recall waking up and seeing all the dregs of drinks left in glasses and polishing them off. I always thought that was such a waste, I mean why pour a drink if you're not going to drink it! I always knew I had a drug problem but didn't think alcohol was an issue. I didn't much like the taste of alcohol but that never stopped me drinking bucket loads of it. I used it to wash the pills down, and I used it when there was nothing else, it was a constant feature. I remember having a huge argument with Neal the next day while we were walking to the beach and not much more.

The next day as planned, off we went to an AA meeting. There were three of us, Sharyn, Neal and me. It reminded me of the meetings I had taken patients to in the past and I didn't hear much of interest. Sharyn got such a fright she packed her bags and went back to Hobart the next day. The tragedy is that several years later she died as a direct result of alcohol. She was found by her six-year-old daughter.

Unbeknown to me the meeting made an impact on Neal and he asked me the following day if I was getting ready for the AA meeting. I said "The AA meeting? I'm not going to the AA meeting, I went last night, I've done my duty, I've taken Sharyn and that's it! I don't need to go!" I remember being horrified at the thought of going to another AA meeting, "Who me, I'm not an alcoholic!" I remember going on and on and protesting profusely. Neal simply said, "Ok if you're not going to go, I'll get a taxi." He didn't drive, I always did the driving no matter what condition I was in, and I always was under the influence of something or other. I thought, if he goes to AA he'll stop drinking, and he'll stop taking drugs and that will leave me on my own and for the first time I thought "What will I do?"

Being on my own had never bothered me before as I'd travelled overseas alone, lived on my own and always felt independent and resourceful but I thought "How am I going to keep this going on my own?" I had felt terribly sick for years and desperately wanted to feel well. If I could have felt well and continued to drink and use drugs I probably would have. So, through gritted teeth I said, "Ok I'll drive you to the meeting." That was two AA meetings in two days now, for other people!

I can't remember what they were saying at that meeting, but I do remember a strong sense of identifying with either what they were saying or how they were saying it and I knew they were talking about me. For the first time in my life, I understood I was one of them and I spent the night in tears. It became apparent to me that I was the one that needed to go to the meetings. I remember through the tears feeling the most enormous weight lift off my shoulders, which I now understand to be a spiritual awakening. The people at the meeting that night were welcoming, kind, and gracious and said "Keep coming back," which I did and continue to do. They said if I didn't have the first drink or the first drug one day at a time I would be in with a chance. The amazing thing that happened when I went to AA is that the desire to drink or use drugs was removed and although there have been times when I've thought about drinking, I've learnt how to deal with that.

By going to AA I've learnt so much about myself, have met some of the most incredible people, and have been able to do so many things I never thought possible. After being in AA for a while I helped a couple of amazing female AA members set up a refuge for alcoholic women and their children in Brisbane. There were refuges for women at the time but none that would take children. It was such a privilege to watch other women recover and to see the impact that had on their children.

My life has changed so much, I've been able to work professionally again and study at university. I'm reliable now and when I travel, I let people know where I'm going and come back when I say I will, even if I don't really want to. In the past I never wanted anyone to know where I was or what I was doing because I knew my life was a sham and although I thought I could control everything; I was often embarrassed by my behaviour. The difference now is I have nothing to hide and that's such a relief.

One of the most extraordinary things I've experienced since being involved in AA is becoming a mother and although my beautiful daughter died far too early, I didn't need to drink or take any drugs. I've learnt that there is nothing more painful than active alcoholism and addiction and that no matter how difficult life becomes for me, taking a drink or drug will not make it any better.

> **Kaz** is a registered nurse working in mental health, drug and alcohol, and sexual health. With 39 years of sobriety in AA she has travelled extensively, returned to study gaining a Masters degree and recently discovered evidence of Tasmanian Aboriginal heritage.

32

Neal Price

By mid 1983 I had been drinking and drugging for over fourteen years and I had pretty well accepted that this would be how my life would continue. My heroes were Janis Joplin and Jimmy Hendrix, both dead before I discovered them in late 1970. I started drinking in 1968 aged fourteen and I still remember the effect it had on me. I drank Stone's Green Ginger Wine in a car in front of the picture theatre at Geeveston in the Huon valley, and after a few mouthfuls, I thought "With this stuff, I can be someone!" It was instant relief, and I really did feel that the alcohol coloured me in. It seemed that the circus had rolled into town, the ferris wheel started moving, the music started up and I had arrived!

Being in a country town, someone that night had thrown a stick of dynamite into the public toilets and pretty soon the police were looking for anyone in a moving car. We were pulled over near the Kermandie Pub and questioned. After only half an hour since my first drink, my attitude was 'cocky', I was smacked in the head with the copper's torch and taken to the police station for my father to collect. I clearly had a personality change, different from my shy school kid demeanour. I went from a shy bookish kid to punk with that one drink.

By age twenty-four the promises alcohol had made had evaporated. The idea that I could 'be someone' using alcohol had faded. I was full of fear and anxiety and the prospects of my holding down a job had vanished. I had lots of sick days and turning up for work became increasingly hard. I moved from Sydney to the Gold Coast, thinking I could escape some of the trouble I was finding myself in.

I told myself I was on an extended holiday. With few resources I survived on the dole and found other opportunistic ways to make money.

My best friend and I were making do with the situation but our lives were almost entirely centred around drinking and taking party drugs. An old friend of mine visited from Tasmania, a girl with whom I had started drinking with at the young age of sixteen. We mostly drank at the inner city Simon's Bistro or the Shipwrights Arms, an old salty's pub in Battery Point. She came from a family of drinkers and had started drinking as early as twelve, a fact she was very proud of.

She worked in a cocktail bar and knew a lot about top shelf drinks and was well versed in drinking a variety of them. We saw her visit as an opportunity to have a party so we bought lots of alcohol and drugs and put her to work making cocktails.

About a week before this, I had been trying to cut back on my drinking but it was awkward, and the few drinks I allowed myself were unsatisfying. I remember thinking to myself, "I won't drink, I won't drink, I won't drink" but I would always start drinking shortly after making this pledge and it left me with a strange dilemma. It hovered like a big question mark over me and I couldn't understand why I had no willpower in this regard, given I was such a wilful person.

My health was also suffering. On a morning walk to the bank to withdraw my last $60, I stopped for a cigarette in the local bus stop a few blocks from my place. I needed Ventolin to have a cigarette. While resting to get strength for the rest of the journey, an elderly man returning from his shopping trip rested in the shelter next to me. He seemed in good condition and I recognised in comparison to this senior person, I was in trouble. While waiting for the bank to open, I remember saying a prayer "God help me, I can't go on living like this. Please help me. I can't go on like this!"

The party started about three o'clock on a Friday afternoon and as people turned up we had many cocktails, mango, strawberry and pineapple daiquiris. By early evening it seemed that everyone was smashed. There were several unknown guests which we overlooked and as the evening progressed, events got more and more out of control. By late evening the mood had changed, fights broke out, the kitchen was broken up and I became violent towards my best friend. I felt deeply ashamed the next morning.

The morning arrived and waking in the wreckage of that party was a complete shock. It was difficult to piece things back together and I had the dreadful realisation I had confronted my neighbours with a few 'home truths'. The vacuum cleaner I had borrowed earlier on the previous day, lay broken at the bottom of the stairwell, where I had thrown it during my outburst.

Flashes of my behaviour kept repeating in my mind. I was full of remorse and guilt.

My friend who was visiting was also in a very odd mood and I had noticed she was drinking furious amounts during the night.

That morning after the party, she had made a suicide attempt by shooting up insulin left in the refrigerator by my mother. This made me angry and it occurred to me that she was an alcoholic. I confronted her and suggested we take her to an AA meeting. I knew from my former years of working as a psychiatric nurse and taking alcoholics to meetings that AA worked for alcoholics. I just didn't believe I was one. She hated the idea but remarkably the three of us somehow attended the Sunday Coolangatta meeting that night.

I had been to AA four years before as part of a stay in rehab but I could not for the life of me understand what these people were talking about. Each person would get up and talk about this mythological last drink they had. They all seemed happy about it but it made no sense to me. So after I left rehab I made a decision to put as much distance between me and AA as I possibly could. I did not want to spend the rest of my life in rooms with these people and I simply couldn't understand why this Last Drink was so important.

Four years later I was on the Gold Coast taking my friend to an AA meeting. My drinking was unstable and as chaotic as ever and I was suffering from a good deal of remorse. Denial was very strong in me. I hadn't put two and two together and thought I could control my drinking and drug taking although I never really had. That was a false belief.

About this time a thought spontaneously occurred to me. It appeared as an external thought, inserted into my mind. Not a thought that I had generated within me. The thought was "You have to go to AA and get sober or else you will die." It was a very small thought and I could have easily ignored it. To this day, I still believe that this was not generated within me and was an external force. It may well have been a spiritual awakening as it seemed completely outside of my control.

Strangely, on this visit to the AA meeting, instead of thinking "What would these people know," which I had thought four years previously, I thought "These people may know something I don't." It changed my life and saved my life. I haven't needed to drink or take drugs since the 15th October 1983.

My friend, the cocktail waitress, freaked out by the meeting, flew back to Tasmania the next day. She continued to drink and drank herself to death six years later. Her six year old daughter tried to wake her alongside an empty bottle of vodka.

A few months before she died I received a late night phone call from her. She was calling a mutual friend and was probably in a blackout. She could not understand how come I was on the phone and was angry and confused and hung up. It was the last time we spoke.

My best friend got sober at the same meeting and we remain sober and life long friends. I've been trained in AA to go to regular and frequent meetings no matter what, and it has stood me in good stead. There are people I love and trust in AA and this has been a remarkable thing for me.

A few things I've heard in AA are "You can leave this meeting and need never drink again if you so choose." That is a critical thing to say, especially to alcoholics who believe they can't stop drinking. Once heard, the alcoholic knows deep down that there is a solution to their addictive drinking. I also heard the phrase "When wrong promptly admit it," and I have found this invaluable. Both of these sayings have directed me through life and uncertain times.

Life hasn't been a bed of roses in sobriety. It took me many years to stabilise my moods from going up and down numerous times a day. I could hardly maintain a constant thought or feeling for a good part of the day. Meetings helped me and I usually found solace listening to the speakers at evening meetings.

Since coming to AA, I have made many good and trustworthy friends, Raucous Dick, Eight O'clock Ross, Adequate from Arncliffe, Sidecar John, Glenda Mary Teresa Langfield Jones, Railway Bill, Bea from Sydney and Ron from Woodridge to name a few.

I'm reminded that Glenda would always say "Get in the middle so when the wolf comes you won't get bitten." I would think, "What's she talking about? There are no wolves in Brisbane," but it's a very useful metaphor. Years later I understood that the 'wolf' is the desire to drink, and the 'middle' is an AA meeting. So to translate that for my slow brain "When the desire to drink returns, be in an AA meeting."

After twenty-seven years in AA I was diagnosed with liver cancer and needed a liver transplant. This was shocking news as I hadn't had a drink for so long but my previous drinking had done a great deal of damage and resulted in tumours in my liver. After almost three years of tests and monitoring I was very ill and lived my life in my apartment in Brisbane. Driving was almost impossible and my car had a series of scrapes and knocks due to my lack of energy and inability to judge the garage and parking spaces.

I received the news on October 11th to go to the hospital as a donor liver had been found. I was extremely nervous and didn't believe I would survive what was ahead of me but I remembered a story told in AA. Ross Fitzgerald's sponsor Lee Parry was about to go into an operation for bowel cancer and he said to his wife Lisa "What will I do?" she replied "Treat it like an adventure Lee." It seemed like a good idea. I held it in my mind as I was wheeled into the operating room.

I received a new liver on October 12th 2009. A nine hour operation completed by a remarkable surgeon Dr Fawcett and team at the Princess Alexandra Hospital in Brisbane. I am forever grateful to them and my donor, a young cyclist who was killed in a hit and run accident in Sale, Victoria.

When I became conscious in the recovery room my first thought was that I had survived. My second thought rang out like a church bell, "Perhaps the problem was in the old liver, perhaps I can drink again." This thought made me sit upright. It arrived in my mind fully dressed. It made itself comfortable and presented its startling epiphany with all the confidence of a trickster with a peanut and three cups.

After all that money and effort to perform the operation, the loss of one man's life, a team of surgeons and nurses in two States, unfathomable hours of training and experience to undertake this miracle, I was considering a drink.

The illness was still active and the alcoholic 'I' was planning to undo the work and investment of a life saving operation. I realised how insane my mind was. It could never be trusted unless I had some kind of help to discipline the way it functioned.

That was twelve years ago. I'm reminded of what my friend Ron from Woodridge would often say, "You don't have to visit Lourdes to witness the miracle of the Holy Waters, because if you're an alcoholic and haven't had a drink for a minute, an hour, a day or 30 years, you're a miracle of AA." AA is full of useful sayings.

Neal is an artist and writer living in Tasmania. He is a transplant recipient and gardener. He has found employment as a teacher, aged care worker, nurse and arts administrator.

The Twelve Steps of Alcoholics Anonymous

1. We admitted we were powerless over alcohol—that our lives had become unmanageable.
2. Came to believe that a Power greater than ourselves could restore us to sanity.
3. Made a decision to turn our will and our lives over to the care of God as we understood Him.
4. Made a searching and fearless moral inventory of ourselves.
5. Admitted to God, to ourselves, and to another human being the exact nature of our wrongs.
6. Were entirely ready to have God remove all these defects of character.
7. Humbly asked Him to remove our shortcomings.
8. Made a list of all persons we had harmed, and became willing to make amends to them all.
9. Made direct amends to such people wherever possible, except when to do so would injure them or others.
10. Continued to take personal inventory and when we were wrong promptly admitted it.
11. Sought through prayer and meditation to improve our conscious contact with God as we understood Him, praying only for knowledge of His will for us and the power to carry that out.
12. Having had a spiritual awakening as the result of these steps, we tried to carry this message to alcoholics and to practice these principles in all our affairs.

How to contact Alcoholics Anonymous

The Australian AA Helpline is 1300 222 222

The Australian AA online meetings: https://meetings.aa.org.au/next/

National Indigenous AA online meetings: https://meetings.aa.org.au/meetings/national-indigenous-aa-online-everywhere-saturday/

www.ingramcontent.com/pod-product-compliance
Ingram Content Group UK Ltd.
Pitfield, Milton Keynes, MK11 3LW, UK
UKHW021326180426
11947UKWH00017B/1471